Glorious Glasgow

James McCarroll and Duncan I. McEwan

Second City of Empire

In many ways 1888 was an *annus mirabilis* for Glasgow. Its world-leading industries were thriving as never before, its population burgeoning, its confidence unrestrained. What made its pre-eminence all the more remarkable was that just a decade before – in 1878 – it had suffered a financial crash of epic proportions: the City of Glasgow Bank, rock-solid pillar of the business establishment, went bust owing the astonishing sum, for the time, of £12 million. The knock-on effect was equally disastrous, with business after business following it into liquidation and several of the bank's ultra-respectable, church-going directors being sent to jail.

The rapid recovery from that disaster was typical of Glasgow's entrepreneurial class, which had consistently demonstrated a capacity to adapt to changing circumstances. Glasgow's first real wave of prosperity, in the eighteenth century, had been fuelled by the importation of tobacco and sugar from the New World. Then when that well ran dry the city moved on to a host of other industries, chief among them cotton manufacturing.

However, it is the indelible imprint of the heavy industries that has characterised Glasgow in the popular imagination. The shipyards, the steel furnaces, the engine works; in the eyes of many these are the city's legacy to the world. Helped by the easy availability of coal and iron ore, men like John Elder, a shipbuilder, William Connal, a pig-iron merchant, Walter Neilson, a railway-engine manufacturer, and William Beardmore, a steel producer, created some of the largest enterprises not just in Britain but also in Europe.

With such economic vigour it is hardly surprising that the population grew exponentially. From just 77,000 in 1801 Glasgow expanded to a metropolis of one million souls by 1912 (perhaps 1.8 million if its district is included). This made it the second-largest city in the United Kingdom and on some estimates the sixth largest in Europe, on a par with the likes of Berlin, Vienna and St Petersburg. Hardly surprising then that Glaswegians proudly referred to the 'dear green place' as the Second City, later adding 'of Empire'.

The municipal fathers were infused with the same dynamism as their counterparts in private enterprise. The council became renowned for its innovations in areas such as water supply, gas, transport and hospitals, although the problems of the slums that blighted the city proved to be significantly more intractable. If there is one initiative that crystallises Glasgow's civic pride it is surely the city chambers on George Square, officially opened in 1888, the extravagant façade surpassed only by the opulence of the interior.

Having achieved such Olympian heights, Glasgow took a collective decision

Sir John Lavery, *State Visit of Her Majesty Queen Victoria to the Glasgow International Exhibition 1888*

to ward off challenges from potential competitors. Its status as the second most important city in the land would be ceded to no one, at least not without a fight. Manchester was its greatest rival and, keen to assert its own credentials, that great Lancastrian redoubt had mounted its Royal Jubilee Exhibition in 1887, an event attended by 4.7 million paying customers. Many in Glasgow saw this as an affront, and, more importantly, as a threat. The city's movers and shakers made plans for the Glasgow International Exhibition. They were determined to surpass Manchester both in the scale and spectacle of the exhibition and also in terms of the numbers who paid to come through the doors.

There was a second reason: Glasgow badly needed a new art gallery, museum and school of art. The space available for the city's extensive, and growing, art collection in the McLellan galleries and in Kelvingrove House (now demolished) was wholly inadequate. It was hoped that if the exhibition turned a healthy profit, it would enable the construction of new facilities for art and design. As one would expect the new Glasgow International Exhibition was flawlessly organised, with an impressive main building designed by the leading Glasgow architect, James Sellars. No less a personage than the Prince of Wales – the future King Edward VII – performed the opening ceremony on 8 May 1888.

The exhibition received an enormous shot in the arm when, in August 1888, Queen Victoria visited on her way to Balmoral. It was her first time in Glasgow since 1849 and the city was beside itself with excitement. The painting on the previous page, by Sir John Lavery, perfectly captures the pomp and circumstance of the Queen's appearance in the main hall. It also worked wonders for the career of John Lavery, who, although born in Belfast, trained at the Glasgow School of Art and later became associated with the movement known as the Glasgow School (colloquially, he was a Glasgow Boy). His huge canvas of the Queen, surrounded by the two hundred and fifty influential people who had gathered to pay homage, firmly established him in the art world and he would become one of Britain's most renowned portrait painters.

It all contributed to the huge success of the exhibition. Glasgow, with 5.7 million people buying tickets – most of them highly impressed by what they had witnessed – easily exceeded Manchester's total. There was enthusiastic support too from the press, which carried endless anecdotes about the goings-on in the west end. Glasgow also achieved its aim of building a new museum and art gallery, sited appropriately at Kelvingrove, although the profits from the exhibition had to be supplemented from private sources and by the ratepayer.

Having made money as the industrial powerhouse par excellence Victorian Glasgow was in the mood to spend it. It was now that the west end came into its own. Men who had made their money in heavy industry, most often in the east of the city, acquired vast new houses in Kelvinside, Dowanhill and in the Park area. A good example of the move west is James Buchanan Mirrlees, who commissioned that fine architect James Boucher to design a house fit for a merchant prince. The result was Redlands House, facing Great Western Road, said to be the largest villa ever built in Kelvinside and surrounded by an estate of twenty-four acres, complete with conservatory, greenhouses and stable block.

Shopping too became essential to the new Glasgow. A range of fashionable emporia – superior to those found in any city in Britain, save London – opened for business. The city centre was well served by outlets that catered to the newly affluent: from Miss Cranston's tearooms to the new phenomenon of the department store, which included legendary Glasgow names like Pettigrew and Stephens, Tréron et Cie and Watt Brothers. However, if one company epitomised the new wave of luxury stores it was Copland and Lye whose sumptuous Caledonian House emporium on Sauchiehall Street was unsurpassed in the range and exclusivity of its offerings.

Sauchiehall and Buchanan streets were the centres of the new consumerism, which, after the economic dynamism of the late Victorian years, peaked in the Edwardian era. The fine painting below (by William Ireland, who also trained at the Glasgow School of Art) of Buchanan Street in 1910, vividly illustrates both the affluence of its shoppers and the quality of its shops in that period.

Glasgow was truly at its zenith.

William Ireland, *Buchanan Street in 1910*

[1] GLASGOW CATHEDRAL, Cathedral Sq. 12th c. There has been a Christian presence here since the 6th c, but the Gothic cathedral we see today can be traced to the late 12th c. Small by some standards, yet elegant and well-proportioned, and according to one historian 'the most important building of its type surviving in Scotland'. The Royal infirmary is on the left and the 1830s Bridge of Sighs, by *David & James Hamilton*, in the foreground.

Cathedral Interior

[2] BLACADER AISLE. This projection from the south transept was added in 1500 by Archbishop Robert Blacader. It was to have been a chapel but only the lower part was completed. The bright-white vaulting and the stone ceiling bosses are exceptional and help to make this the brightest part of the cathedral.

[3] ST MUNGO'S TOMB. St Kentigern (or Mungo), the patron saint of Glasgow, was the first bishop in the kingdom of Strathclyde and is said to have been much loved by the common people. He died c. AD 612 and his tomb is at the heart of the crypt in the lower church.

[4] The stained glass is splendid throughout, none more so than these windows of the 1950s, which represent the various crafts of Glasgow, and were donated by the Trades House of Glasgow to replace windows of 1860.

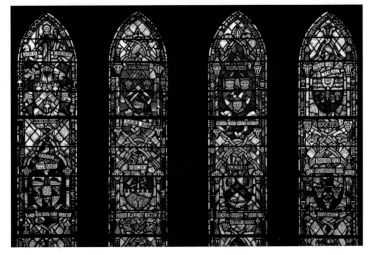

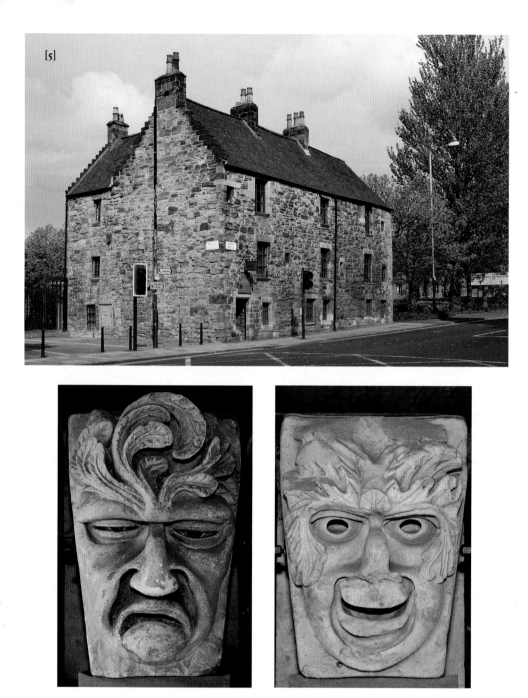

[5] PROVAND'S LORDSHIP, 1471, 3 Castle St, opp. Cathedral Sq. Built as a home for the chaplain of the adjacent St Nicholas hospital (now lost), Provand's Lordship is said to be the oldest house in Glasgow. The word Provand derives from the prebend of Balornock, who also resided here. Restored to former glories in 1906 by the Provand's Lordship Society, the house is now a museum. There is a fine collection of 17th c. furniture, some of it donated by Sir William Burrell, as well as fine artworks. [6a and 6b] TONTINE FACES, c. 1740–60 St Nicholas Garden, behind Provand's Lordship. The faces are sandstone effigies carved by Mungo Naismith and others, used as keystones on Glasgow town hall (later the Tontine hotel) on Trongate. Following demolition work, the Faces were scattered across the city but thanks to the sterling work of 1930s Glasgow journalist James Cowan (pen name Peter Prowler) they have been reunited.

[7] BARONY CHURCH, 1889, 1 Castle St, *Sir J. J. Burnet & John Campbell*. This fine red-sandstone church by competition winners Burnet and Campbell replaced an earlier Gothic church of 1798. It has a front based on Dunblane's cathedral but an interior similar to Glasgow's. It is now a ceremonial hall for Strathclyde University.

[8] GLASGOW EVANGELICAL CHURCH, 14 Cathedral Sq. 1880, *John Honeyman*. This fine Italianate structure in blond sandstone was formerly known as Barony North church. After falling into disrepair, it was taken over by the Glasgow Evangelical Church (watchwords 'independent, Protestant and Reformed') in 1972 and painstakingly restored by the congregation. **[9]** The splendid church organ, built by Forster and Andrews of Hull in 1887, is listed by the British Institute of Organ Studies as an 'instrument of importance to the national heritage'. The colonnaded vestibule, gallery stairway, pulpit and curved stairway are also worthy of note.

NECROPOLIS, 1833, adjacent to cathedral. Modelled on the Père Lachaise graveyard in Paris, the necropolis was a garden before being redeveloped by the Merchants' House of Glasgow. Many of the tombs [see 12–17] are architectural marvels.

[10] ENTRANCE FAÇADE

[11] NECROPOLIS GATES, 1833

[12] AITKEN OF DALMOAK MAUSOLEUM, the largest in the necropolis.

[13] MAJOR ARCHIBALD MONTEATH MAUSOLEUM, notable for its many faces.

[14] JAMES BUCHANAN OF DOWANHILL, one of the city's leading businessmen.

[15] JOHN KNOX MONUMENT: the twelve-foot statue of the great Protestant reformer, mounted on a Doric column, dominates its surroundings.

[16] ALEXANDER MCCALL, former city chief constable: Celtic cross by Charles Rennie Mackintosh, who was a friend of the McCall family.

[17] CHARLES TENNANT: the great industrialist's chemical works in St Rollox, Glasgow was the biggest in the world.

[18] ST MUNGO MUSEUM OF RELIGIOUS LIFE AND ART, 2 Castle St. 1989, *Ian Begg*. On the site of the former Bishop's castle, the museum has two displays on world religions and one on religion in Scotland, while outside we find Britain's first Zen garden. To the side, *James Miller*'s Royal infirmary, a replacement of the 1900s for *Robert Adam*'s much-loved hospital of 1792.

[19] KING WILLIAM II OF SCOTLAND (III OF ENGLAND) STATUE, Cathedral Sq, 1735, *probably by Peter Scheemakers*. The bronze statue of King William (1650–1702) was moved here from Trongate in 1926. The King is depicted as a Roman general and the tail of his horse has a ball-joint, enabling it to twist in the wind.

[20] BLIND ASYLUM, 1879, *William Landless* and ROYAL INFIRMARY, 1914, *James Miller*, Castle St. Landless's building (*left*) in the Franco-Flemish style with its dominant spire and carvings became part of the Royal in 1940. Miller's hospital (*right*) was not universally popular, with critics opining that it overwhelmed the medieval cathedral.

[21] MARTYRS' SCHOOL, Parson St. 1895, *Charles Rennie Mackintosh*. Named for three Covenanters who were executed nearby, in 1684, this is one of Mackintosh's first major works. Note the art nouveau features around the windows and doors, adumbrating later themes.

[22] Charles Rennie Mackintosh was actually born in Parson Street, Townhead, in 1868, as the plaque records. After training at the Glasgow School of Art and as an apprentice architect, Mackintosh joined the Glasgow firm of Honeyman and Keppie. Although some of his most acclaimed designs were conceived here he was never fully appreciated by his native city and he left Glasgow in 1913. The father of the 'Glasgow Style' movement, Mackintosh is now rightly regarded as one of the twentieth century's greatest architects and designers.

[23] These sculptures (in nearby St Mungo Place) commemorate Mackintosh's unique design style.

[24]

[25]

[26]

[27]

[28]

[29]

[24] CHRIST ON THE CROSS, St Mungo's, Parson St.

[25] CHRIST HEALING A BLIND BOY, 92 Castle St. 1881, *Charles Grassby*. A poignant scene on the façade of the former blind asylum with the kneeling blind boy caught in the act of prayer.

[26] QUEEN VICTORIA, Royal infirmary, s. façade, 1914, *Albert Hemstock Hodge.*

[27] DAVID LIVINGSTONE, Cathedral Sq. 1879, *John Mossman and others*. A naturalistic interpretation of the great explorer, missionary and anti-slavery campaigner, who was born in Blantyre in 1813. During one of his many epic expeditions in Africa, he was tracked down by journalist H. M. Stanley, who uttered the immortal words 'Dr Livingstone I presume'. Statue has interesting pictorial reliefs.

[28] LADY WELL, Ladywell St. In medieval times, this was used by the common people, who were not permitted to use the priests' well nearby.

[29] ALLEGORICAL FEMALE FIGURE, 215 High St. 1895, plaque: *William Salmon*; sculptor of statue unknown.

[30] GIANT SAFETY PIN, Strathclyde Uni. 1996, *George Wyllie*. The official name for the seven-metre-tall nappy pin is *Mthothta*, Greek for maternity.

[31] ROTTENROW MATERNITY HOSPITAL, Rottenrow, 1879, *Robert Baldie*. These arches are all that remain of Glasgow's famous maternity hospital, which operated here for 130 years.

[30]

[31]

[32] TOLBOOTH STEEPLE, Glasgow Cross, 1626, *John Boyd*. The former 17th c. municipal buildings here were gradually swept away, leaving only the steeple with its 'splendid verticality'. To the left is the west quadrant, an arc of 1922 (*A. Graham Henderson*), part of an unrealised plan to complete the Cross

[33] MERCAT CROSS AND MERCAT BUILDING, Glasgow Cross, 1930, *Edith Burnet Hughes*. A reinterpretation of the 17th c. style of market cross, and behind it the Mercat building of 1928 with its Ionic columns, also by *A. Graham Henderson*.

[34] THE HIGH COURT OF JUSTICIARY, Saltmarket, 1814, *William Stark*. According to Pevsner this is 'the purest piece of Greek Revival in Glasgow, and among the first of this monumental size and purity in Britain'. It functioned not only as a court but also comprised municipal offices and a jail. Remodelled in 1845 and then reconstructed as a court building alone in 1910–13.

[35] HIGH COURT EXTENSION, 1997. The court was extended into Mart Street and the complex now comprises seven courtrooms.

[36] GALLERY OF MODERN ART, Royal Exchange Sq. 1832, *David Hamilton*. Originally a grand mansion of 1770 for tobacco lord William Cunninghame of Lainshaw and much admired by the people of Glasgow, who considered it the finest urban house in Scotland. After Cunninghame's death it was owned for a time by the Royal Bank of Scotland but was then brilliantly converted by Hamilton in the Graeco-Roman style, becoming known as the Royal Exchange. Thanks to the imposing portico, the huge Corinthian columns and the magnificent cupola it is one of the most-admired and recognisable structures in the city, a testament to Hamilton's undoubted genius. It has had several uses down the centuries but today is an art gallery operated by the council, with a library in the basement. The elegant interior – note especially the beautiful ceiling and the fluted columns – was inspired by Sir John Soane's Bank of England. Viewed to best effect from Ingram St.

[37] ARCHES, Royal Exchange Sq/ Royal Bank Pl. 1827. The triumphal arches to either side of the former bank building [see **38**] lead us from Buchanan St. into Glasgow's historic Merchant City.

[38] FORMER BANK BUILDING, Royal Exchange Sq. 1827, *Archibald Elliot II*. Another fine Greek Revival design, influenced by the work of Elliot's father, also an architect. It complements the adjacent Royal Exchange, and is striking in its night attire. The frontage onto Buchanan St. was added by Charles Wilson in 1852.

[39] CORINTHIAN CLUB, 191 Ingram St. 1841/1879, *David Hamilton*/façade *John Burnet*. Hamilton designed this building for the Union Bank but the elaborate façade was added by Burnet. Renamed Lanarkshire House, it was later used as a criminal court and today is an upmarket restaurant/bar. Classical figures and representations of Scottish towns on the façade.

[40] ST DAVID (RAMSHORN), 98 Ingram St. 1826, *Thomas Rickman*. Built to replace an earlier church here. The main body is T-plan, in the style of the Scottish Gothic Revival, with a very tall tower. As with many other notable Glasgow buildings it is the focal point of a street, in this case Candleriggs.

[41] HUTCHESONS' HALL, 158 Ingram St. 1805, *David Hamilton*. The philanthropic Hutcheson brothers, George and Thomas, rose to prominence during the 17th c. Their original hospital was located in Trongate but Hamilton was commissioned by the trustees to design a new facility, and the result was one of Glasgow's most iconic buildings.

[42] FORMER BANKING HALL, Ingram St/Glassford St. 1900, *Sir J. J. Burnet*. An extension to the Glassford St. head office of the former Glasgow Savings Bank. The architect was John James Burnet, son of John Burnet, who was responsible for the head office. The French Renaissance style of Burnet *fils* contrasts markedly with Burnet *pere*'s three-storey Italianate design. The dome and external sculptures catch the eye.

[43] ITALIAN CENTRE, John St. with Ingram St. façade, 1989, *Page and Park*. A terrace of warehouses that has transmogrified into Glasgow's 'mini-Milan' complete with designer clothes shops, much favoured by Old Firm footballers. The pavement cafés give the piazza a Continental feel although the Glasgow weather sometimes fails to cooperate.

[44] FORMER NEWSPAPER OFFICES AND PRINT WORKS, 145 Albion St. 1936, *Sir Owen Williams*. Built for the then highly influential *Daily Express* and based on that organ's famous offices in Fleet Street with its opaque glass and black Vitrolite frontage. Now flats and offices.

[45] JOHN STREET CHURCH, 1860, *J. T. Rochead*. Built for the United Presbyterians. Superb design with the undoubted highlight being the double-height, principal floor with colonnade of Ionic columns and glass fitted directly into it, a remarkable experiment in fenestration. Rochead would later design that icon of the Scottish nation, the Wallace monument, near Stirling.

[46] CITY HALLS, Candleriggs, from 1817, *James Cleland*. The council used this for official functions from 1841. There are five halls, including the impressive grand hall, which at one time could accommodate 3,500 guests. It was here that Dickens gave his celebrated readings, Thackeray lectured and Dr Livingstone was honoured. Recently refurbished and now used mainly for concerts.

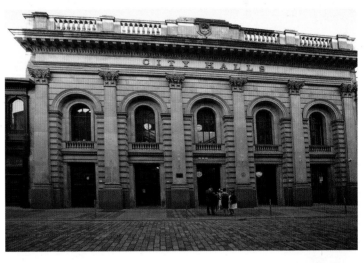

[47] TOBACCO MERCHANT'S HOUSE, 42 Miller St. 1775, *John Craig*. The oldest house in the Merchant City, one of a number of detached villas on Miller Street, most of which were considerably larger than Craig's property. Restored in 1995, it now provides office space.

[48] TRADES HALL, 85 Glassford St. 1794, *Robert Adam*. The last surviving Adam façade in Glasgow. Palladian in style with characteristic flourishes, such as the splendid Ionic centrepiece and the large dome, it ranks among the great Scottish architect's finest work. Built for the Trades' House, which at one time controlled the city's trades.

[49] TRADES HALL INTERIOR. The Trades House organisation is now a charity and the impressive seventy-foot pilastered hall is today used for a variety of events and functions.

[50] COUNTY BUILDINGS, 40 Wilson St. 1844, *Clarke & Bell*. Competition winners Clarke & Bell established themselves in Glasgow with this design and their massive building occupies an entire street block. The south face (*shown here*) has a giant Greek-style portico with six columns sitting on a plinth. It once housed municipal offices, courts and cells. [51] COUNTY BUILDINGS, west façade. This section of the county buildings, with its fine Corinthian columns, was occupied by the Merchants' House and faces the Trades Hall down Garth Street.

[52] FRUIT MARKET, Bell St/Candleriggs 1902, *A. B. McDonald*. Executed by city engineer McDonald in a style known as Edwardian Renaissance.

[53] FRUIT MARKET INTERIOR. Today known as Merchant Square, the airy and stylish interior plays host to bars and restaurants.

[54] BABBITY BOWSTER BISTRO, 16 Blackfriars St. 1792/reconstructed 1985 by *Nicholas Groves-Raines*. This charming bistro is the last relic of an ambitious late 18th c. plan by the Adam brothers to lay out a new thoroughfare, Stirling Street, and an associated square. Parts of the building (attributed by some to *Robert Adam* himself) are original, for example the Roman Doric doorway, while others are new but based on the old design. The bar has a panel showing a kilted Scot performing the babbity bowster, a country dance.

[55] CROWN ARCADE, 31–35 Virginia St. 1819. Virginia St. was laid out by tobacco merchant Andrew Buchanan in 1753 and the arcade here was Glasgow's tobacco exchange, as the blue plaque on the wall indicates. Courtyard area completely remodelled in 2007.

[56] BRITANNIA PANOPTICON MUSIC HALL, 113 Trongate, 1857, *Thomas Gildard and others*. Occupying the top two floors of what was originally a warehouse, this is the second oldest theatre in Scotland and the oldest surviving music hall in the world. Among the notables who trod its boards were Stan Laurel and Sir Harry Lauder. Exterior recently restored to former glories.

[57] TRON STEEPLE, 71 Trongate, tower 1592, spire 1636, arches 1855. The original church was St Mary and St Anne, founded in 1484. Neglected after the Reformation but rebuilt in 1592, latterly becoming the Tron kirk because the tron, or public-weighing apparatus, was stored in its basement. The kirk was burnt to the ground in 1793 by the notorious Hellfire club, leaving only the steeple we see here. The church was rebuilt in 1794 by *James Adam* – set back from the steeple – and is now the Tron theatre.

[58] SALTMARKET. An important street dating back to the Middle Ages, once known as Waulkergait. A fashionable place to live in the 18th c. but like the rest of this quarter lost much of its lustre as affluent Glasgow moved west.

[59] DUKE OF WELLINGTON STATUE, Queen St. 1844, *Baron Marochetti*. This fine equestrian statue, in bronze, is invariably decorated with traffic cones, a practice deplored by officialdom, but seen by many as the perfect example of Glasgow humour. Born in Dublin, Arthur Wellesley, Duke of Wellington, defeated Emperor Napoleon at Waterloo in 1815 and became prime minister in 1828. The decision by Glasgow to award the commission to Marochetti was a controversial one, not least because he had designed Napoleon's mausoleum in Paris. However, the quality of the design, with Wellington seated on his charger, Copenhagen, is surely beyond criticism.

[60] This narrative frieze, 'The Soldier's Return', like Marochetti's others on the Duke's statue, is well worth examining.

[61] FRUIT BOWL, This highly appropriate piece can be seen on the roof of the fruit market, on Bell St/Candleriggs [see **52** and **53**].

[62] ST MUNGO, former banking hall, Ingram St.
George Frampton.

[63] MERCURIUS, Italian centre, Ingram St.
Alexander Stoddart.

[64] GEORGE HUTCHESON, Hutchesons' hall, Ingram St. *James Colquhoun.*

[65] FRIEZE, county buildings, Wilson St. *Walter Buchan* and *John Mossman* [see **50**].

Architectural Genius

Glasgow, declared John Betjeman, is the finest Victorian city in Britain and who could disagree with that assessment? A combination of huge wealth and a generation of architects with sublime talents delivered a collection of buildings that are outstanding by any standards. Yet Glasgow is about much more than Victoriana. There are still substantial parts of the old medieval burgh extant, not to mention the Georgian splendour on Blythswood Hill, in parts of the Merchant City and on the banks of the Clyde. Little wonder that Glasgow was named UK City of Architecture and Design in 1999.

Although fine practitioners were at work before him – consider for example the splendid Trades hall of 1794 by Robert Adam, the greatest of all Scottish architects – the founding father of Glasgow architecture was surely David Hamilton (1768–1843). His legacy to the city cannot be underestimated and includes three of its most iconic structures: Hutchesons' hall, the Royal Exchange and the Western club.

Hamilton's influence did not die with him. His pupils carried on his legacy, most prominent among them Charles Wilson, who not only designed many superb buildings but was also responsible for what is frequently described as the finest example of town planning in Britain: the Park Terrace and Park Circus enclave atop Woodlands Hill (*see photo on facing page*).

As the century progressed many more influential firms opened for business. One of the most important was the practice founded in 1844 by John Burnet, a busy and admired architect who designed a wide variety of buildings in a range of styles. By 1880, Burnet had been joined by two brilliant practitioners: his son, J. J. Burnet, and John Campbell. Burnet and Co had many distinguished contemporaries: William Leiper, William Clarke, George Bell, Alexander Kirkland and the erudite and scholarly John Honeyman, who scaled new peaks with his superb church plans.

However, the leading practice in Victorian Glasgow was that set up in 1849 by Alexander Thomson, although the pity is that many of his wonderful creations have been demolished while others are in a shocking state of repair. Yet 'Greek' Thomson's contribution to Glasgow and more broadly to the built form is immeasurable and for confirmation one need look no further than his St Vincent Street church, surely among the finest in Europe. Many tried to copy his unique style, before and after his death. None succeeded.

There is of course a Glasgow architect whose fame has all but eclipsed his wonderfully talented predecessors. His name is Charles Rennie Mackintosh, a man whose sublime vision has raised him to the pantheon that includes such illustrious names as Frank Lloyd Wright, Le Corbusier and Walter Gropius. Mackintosh was born in Glasgow, in Parson Street, and, in 1884, at the age of sixteen, was articled to John Hutchison before moving to the firm of

Charles Rennie Mackintosh   *Alexander 'Greek' Thomson*

Honeyman and Keppie. At night he studied at the Glasgow School of Art, which was then headed by the most important director in its history, Francis Henry 'Fra' Newbery, who quickly recognised the young man's genius not just in architecture but also in painting, interior design and furniture-making. Mackintosh was also greatly assisted by the award of a scholarship to study abroad; it had been established to honour the memory of his most eminent antecedent, one Alexander 'Greek' Thomson.

Mackintosh's masterwork also happens to be his alma mater, the Glasgow School of Art, built in two phases between 1898 and 1909. Rejecting the Victorian fixation with the past, and styles such as Classicism and Gothic, he conceived a truly modern building, an eclectic mix drawn from many styles: art nouveau, the Arts and Crafts movement, and, in its first phase, even the Scottish vernacular tradition of the sixteenth and seventeenth centuries. As the *Daily Telegraph* recently noted, 'No building in Britain more powerfully exemplifies architecture as a total work of art.'

Any account of the buildings of the late nineteenth century must acknowledge the role of the architectural sculpture. It seems every great building of the period had to be adorned either by statues of artists and writers or by allegorical figures linking a commercial enterprise with noble virtues. John Mossman's carvings and statues appear on an enormous number of public buildings, perhaps finding their finest expression on the former St Andrew's halls, now the Mitchell library. Others made a huge contribution: William Birnie Rhind, William Kellock Brown and John Derwent Wood, to name but three.

Great architecture did not die out with the coming of the twentieth century. Sir J. J. Burnet continued to produce notable designs as did the likes of James Salmon. The most distinguished name from this period was arguably James Miller, who had come to prominence thanks largely to his railway-station designs but was prolific in a wide range of other forms. Perhaps his greatest legacy is the 1927 Bank of Scotland at 110 St Vincent Street, an awe-inspiring monument to Mammon that conjures up New York and Chicago.

As Glasgow's suburbs continued to expand there was a corresponding boom in church building in the years to 1960. The most-renowned ecclesiastical architect of the period was Jack Coia, who was heavily patronised by the Roman Catholic Church. This was also an era for which the architectural sculpture was crucial and the carvings on the churches are often works of art in their own right.

After the architectural brutalism of much of the 1960s and 1970s there has been a welcome return to thoughtful design in the twenty-first century. Offices, churches and houses display a genuine vitality, a new spirit that has done much to help the regeneration of areas such as the Gorbals, which has been utterly transformed. The new generation of architects has produced impressive work: five recent Glasgow buildings have won the prestigious Andrew Doolan Best Building in Scotland award, presented by the Royal Incorporation of Architects: the Clavius building on Hill Street (2004), which is shown below; the restoration of Castlemilk stables (2008); the small-animal hospital on

Garscube estate (2009), seamlessly integrated with its natural environment; the striking extension to the housing association offices on Pettigrew Street (2010); Maggie's centre at Gartnavel hospital (2012).

There has also been a welcome renaissance in public art, including the architectural sculpture, and in particular the work of Andy Scott – he of Heavy Horse fame – has captured the popular imagination.

Clavius building

[66] CITY CHAMBERS, George Sq. 1890, *William Young*. The magnificent city chambers (*centre*) leave no one in any doubt about Glasgow's Victorian prominence and competition-winner Young's Venetian-inspired design fits the wide expanse of the square perfectly. In the foreground, we have the 1838 statue of Sir Walter Scott, the first erected anywhere in the world to the great novelist, designed by *John Greenshields* but carved after his death by *John Ritchie*. Quite appropriately, Scott is holding a pen in his left hand and a book in his right. To the right, the former GPO building of 1878 by *Robert Mathieson*, later extended down to Ingram St.

[67] GEORGE SQUARE looking west. Scotland's best-known square was named after George III and first laid out in 1781. Between 1787 and the 1820s its borders were filled up with elegant three-storey houses with a private garden, fenced off, in the centre. However, by the mid-19th c. it had become almost completely commercial, home to banks and hotels and later the city chambers. Today it is the heart of Glasgow and continues to host any number of important events. The building behind the tour bus is the Merchants' House.

[68] CENOTAPH, 1924, slab – *Sir J. J. Burnet*; lions and St Mungo statue – *Ernest Gillick*. Glasgow's tribute to the brave soldiers, sailors and airmen who fell in the First World War and in other conflicts.

City Chambers

[69] JUBILEE PEDIMENT, main façade, *George Anderson Lawson* (modeller). Completed in 1887, the fiftieth anniversary of Queen Victoria's accession as monarch, this intricate confection shows her on the throne, surrounded by subjects from all four corners of the world and other symbols of Empire.

[70] CENTRAL TOWER. A very tall and imposing focal point, which some argue references the tower on 'Greek' Thomson's St Vincent Street church, topped off by a fine cupola. The new city chambers did much to restore Glasgow's usual self-confidence after the disastrous collapse of the City of Glasgow Bank in 1878 and such was the public's enthusiasm that four hundred thousand people attended a ten-day viewing.

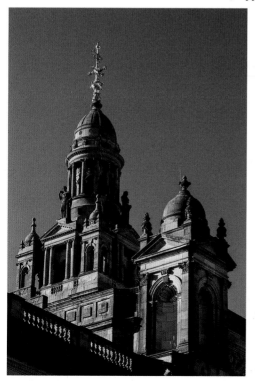

[71] JOHN STREET FAÇADE. These imposing arches link Young's original building with the east block, completed in 1923.

City Chambers Interiors, George Square

[72] BANQUETING HALL. This huge space, double-height and barrel-vaulted, carries the influence of the French Renaissance. Replete with art works, including several by the Glasgow Boys. The medieval scene is *The Granting of Glasgow's Charter by William the Lion* by George Henry. Glasgow's coat of arms is in the central panel below.

[73] MARBLE STAIRCASES. The exterior is richly detailed but it is surpassed by the astonishing opulence of the interior, for which only the finest materials were used. The exquisite marble staircases with their wonderful columns are an obvious example but there are many others: the vaulted ceilings; the floors with their intricate mosaics; the marvellous tapestries and wall-coverings; the lavish plasterwork; the mahogany and walnut finishes.

[74] CEILINGS. The lavishly decorated ceilings are another notable feature, and the circular opening shows two of them to good effect.

George Square Statuary

[75] QUEEN VICTORIA, 1854, *Baron Marochetti*. Victoria's first visit to Glasgow in 1849 was deemed so momentous that it prompted the city elite to commission a statue from Marochetti. No expense was spared, with only the finest bronze and granite used. Such was the excitement generated that when the completed work was unveiled (at its original home on the junction of St Vincent Pl. and Buchanan St.) tens of thousands of cheering Glaswegians turned out. The Queen is seated side-saddle and is holding an imperial sceptre.

[76] PRINCE ALBERT, 1866, *Baron Marochetti*. Following the premature death of Albert, Prince Consort, in 1861, Glasgow once again turned to Marochetti. His 'Albert' was placed in George Square in 1866, at which time the statue of his wife, Queen Victoria, was relocated there in order that the couple who were so devoted in life would forever be together.

George Square Statuary

[77]

[78]

[77] ROBERT BURNS, 1877, *George Ewing*. Born in Alloway, the son of a poor tenant farmer, Burns (1759–96) was lionised following the publication of his first collection of verse in 1786. The Ploughman Poet is undoubtedly the greatest literary figure Scotland has ever produced. Note the bonnet in his right hand and the daisy in his left.

[78] JAMES WATT, 1830, *Francis Chantrey*. Greenock-born Watt (1736–1819) has become synonymous with the steam engine and his pioneering work was central to the Industrial Revolution. In his right hand he is holding compasses, while in his left there is a drawing of a steam engine.

[79] WILLIAM GLADSTONE, 1902, *William Thornycroft*. Born in Liverpool to a wealthy Scottish merchant, Gladstone (1809–98) was prime minister on four occasions. His statue has a peculiar detail: the forefinger of his left hand looks as if it is stuck in a book, but this was a device to hide the fact that he lost the digit in a shooting accident.

Merchants' House, George Sq/West George St. 1877
John Burnet

[**80**] MERCHANTS' HALL. The Merchants' House of Glasgow is one of the most important organisations in the city, tracing its history back to the sixteenth century. It now sits proudly on the edge of George Sq, from where it administers its many charitable trusts. The interior, as one would expect, is ornate with fine portraits of prominent merchants.

[**81**] DOME. The short dome, at the corner, is enhanced by a model of a merchant ship under full sail, an appropriate symbol for an organisation representing the commercial classes of the city. In fact, the exterior as a whole is distinguished by the generous use of sculpture.

[**82**] CORBEL, east elevation. The relaxed-looking figures (*James Young*, sculptor) supporting the corbel are beautifully done – and easily missed by failing to look up!

[83] COUNTING HOUSE PUB, St Vincent Pl/George Sq. 1870, *J. T. Rochead*. The former bank is now a pub and the huge banking hall is one of the most convivial watering holes in the city. The shield above the main entrance on St Vincent Pl, supported by two mythical figures, is the most prominent exterior feature.

[84] ANCHOR LINE BUILDING, 12 St Vincent Pl. 1907, *James Miller*. The Anchor Line was one of the most important companies operating on the transatlantic routes and its first Glasgow–New York steamship put to sea in 1856. Many of its ships were built at the company's yard in Meadowside, where the Clyde and Kelvin converge. The line was bought by Cunard in 1911. Masonry on façade is white Doulton Carrara.

[85] FORMER EVENING CITIZEN BUILDING, 24 St Vincent Pl. 1889, *T. L. Watson*. Founded in 1864 the *Evening Citizen* was Glasgow's first evening newspaper, and, with its Unionist politics, had a decidedly conservative tinge. It became known to many as the churchgoer's paper thanks to its ecclesiastical notices and stories. Publication ceased in 1974. The acclaimed building is of red Mauchline sandstone, with fine corbelled clock tower, deeply recessed windows and rich carvings.

[86] CLYDESDALE BANK, 30–40 St Vincent Pl. 1874, *John Burnet*. An exuberant palazzo with fine statuary and carvings, the architect's original symmetrical conception was stymied by the development of the *Citizen* building next door [see **85**].

[87] SCOTTISH PROVIDENT INSTITUTION, 17–29 St Vincent Pl. 1908, *J. M. Peddie*. This huge building confirms St Vincent Place's importance in the commercial life of Victorian and Edwardian Glasgow.

[88] QUEEN STREET STATION, interior. Glasgow's oldest surviving major station serves destinations to the east and north, esp. the inter-city line to Edinburgh, one of the busiest in the UK. Journeys here end dramatically, in a half-mile of tunnel, before one emerges into a shed with an imposing arched roof.

[89] FORMER LIBERAL CLUB, Buchanan St/Nelson Mandela Pl, 1909, *A. N. Paterson*. This sandstone giant was built to eclipse the Conservative club on Bothwell St. There was great rivalry between the two parties and until the outbreak of the Great War in 1914 the Liberals and Conservatives dominated Glasgow politics. Later became the Royal Scottish Academy of Music and Drama, which also encompassed the Athenaeum building (*left*), before becoming a commercial outlet. The huge cast-iron windows rise through two storeys at first-floor level.

[90] ATHENAEUM, Nelson Mandela Pl. 1886, *Sir J. J. Burnet*. Founded as a private commercial college in 1847, the Athenaeum organisation is an excellent example of Victorian self-help. Its move here enabled the provision of lecture theatres and other facilities for the two thousand students. On the façade, four Ionic columns supporting Flaxman, Wren, Purcell and Reynolds.

[91] ST GEORGE'S TRON,
165 Buchanan St. 1809, *William Stark*. On an island with the adjoining Nelson Mandela Place, the eclectic design, with hints of the great English architects Hawksmoor and Wren, makes this a most recognisable church. The four finials were to have been statues but finances dictated otherwise.

[92] STOCK EXCHANGE,
159 Buchanan St. 1877, *John Burnet*. This stretch of Buchanan St/Nelson Mandela Pl. has a plethora of superb buildings and the Gothic lines of Burnet's former stock exchange are no exception. It is one of the most distinctive structures in Glasgow. Extension in Nelson Mandela Pl. The interior was removed in 1971 and replaced by office accommodation. It no longer functions as a stock exchange.

[93] ROYAL FACULTY OF PROCURATORS, 12 Nelson Mandela Pl. 1856, *Charles Wilson*. Procurators represented clients in the lower courts and the Faculty, which dates back to the 17th c, still looks after the interests of Glasgow solicitors. Wilson's design (*left*) is Venetian Renaissance, and boasts an array of lawyerly sculptured heads above the lower windows. St George's Tron is in the centre.

[94] FORMER WESTERN CLUB, 147 Buchanan St. 1842, *David & James Hamilton*. Founded in 1825, this is the oldest gentleman's club in Glasgow and at its peak had six hundred members. The Hamiltons' magnificent Italianate palazzo was influenced by their Continental sojourns and its interior (now an Apple store, the club having moved) was in its day the nonpareil of comfort.

[95] THE LIBRARY, ROYAL FACULTY OF PROCURATORS. Quite simply, one of the most elegant spaces in Glasgow. Large Venetian windows at each end. The superb square piers divide the room into nave and aisles and the busts of law lords and distinguished lawyers are a perfect adornment.

[96] GLASGOW ROYAL CONCERT HALL. *1990, Sir Leslie Martin/* STATUE OF DONALD DEWAR 2002, *Kenny Mackay*, corner Buchanan St/Sauchiehall St. With a main auditorium of 2,500 seats, this is the city's main venue for the classical repertoire. In 1993 Nelson Mandela received awards here. Donald Dewar was Scotland's first First Minister and the man many credit with the establishment of the Scottish Parliament in 1999.

[97] BUCHANAN STREET, LOOKING SOUTH. This street in the heart of the city, with its huge range of retail outlets, is Scotland's premier shopping destination and millions have been spent to retain that cherished status. In the centre, in green, we see Buchanan St. underground station.

[98] ROGANO'S OYSTER BAR, 11 Exchange Pl. 1936, *Weddell & Inglis*. This art deco gem with its giant lobster and Vitrolite panelling has been a Glasgow style icon for decades. The interior brings to mind a Cunard liner from the golden age of cruising. Specialises in seafood.

[99] PRINCES SQUARE,
48 Buchanan St. 1842, *John Baird*.
What was once a business chambers,
stable and coach house has been, since
1988, one of the most stylish shopping
experiences in the country. The
ironwork, balconies, curved stairs and
glass lifts create a Parisian feel. Named
for the Prince of Wales, who later
became Edward VII.

**[100] FORMER MISS CRANSTON'S
TEAROOM,** 91 Buchanan St. 1896,
George Washington Browne. Kate
Cranston's third Glasgow tearoom and
her most celebrated thanks to the sheer
genius of the interior designers: George
Walton and Charles Rennie Mackintosh.
It was the start of a fruitful business
relationship between the teashop legend
and Mackintosh and her patronage was
crucial for his finances. Sadly, there are
now no traces of either Walton or
Mackintosh, but the fine Dutch-style
exterior is extant, topped by a gable
with an unusual shape.

[101] ARGYLL ARCADE,
30 Buchanan St. 1827, *John Baird*.
Hosting thirty or so diamond dealers
and jewellers, this L-shaped building is
often referred to as the Hatton Garden
of Scotland. It is one of the oldest
arcades in Europe, with glass roof and
hammer beams. Connects Buchanan
St. with Argyle St.

[102] FRASER'S, 45 Buchanan St. Glasgow's grandest department store has steadily expanded along Buchanan St. over the years, absorbing rival shops and now comprises five buildings. The company was founded by Hugh Fraser in 1849 and after rapid expansion would become the retail empire, House of Fraser. It now owns sixty stores the length and breadth of Britain.

[103] FORMER BOAC BUILDING, 85 Buchanan St. 1970, *Gillespie, Kidd & Coia*. One of the most unusual buildings here, the copper-clad façade nevertheless complements its more traditional stone-built neighbours.

[104] BANK EXTENSION, 113–115 Buchanan St. 1888, *A. Sydney Mitchell*. Despite its impressive domed tower and dimensions this is an extension to David Rhind's bank (*left*) of 1857, which is at 8 Gordon Street [see 138].

CITY CHAMBERS CARVINGS, George Sq. There are many intricate carvings on the exterior, including [105] THE ARTS OF PEACE, *John Mossman*, which is on the very interesting George St. façade. The figure on the left is weaving, the one on the right is writing, while the main, central figure is holding a corn stalk, and [106] ALLEGORICAL FIGURES, *unknown*. In a building of this size and complexity a significant numbers of sculptors were employed, most of them chosen by architect William Young. They were all fine artists, the likes of Charles Grassby, John Mossman, George Anderson Lawson and John Rhind notable among them.

CLYDESDALE BANK, St Vincent Pl, 1874. Heavily ornamented exterior [see 86] in the Venetian style, typical of architect Sir J. J. Burnet in this period: [107] FATHER CLYDE, *Charles Grassby*, located in the keystone, and [108] TRADE, *John Mossman*. Female figure holding an olive branch stands above a cloth seller, who is probably of Middle Eastern origin.

[107]   [108]

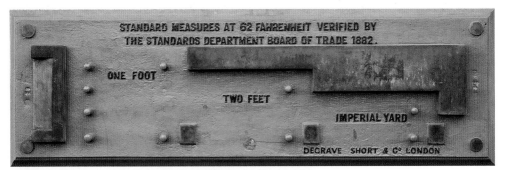

STANDARD MEASURES AT 62 FAHRENHEIT VERIFIED BY
THE STANDARDS DEPARTMENT BOARD OF TRADE 1882.

ONE FOOT

TWO FEET

IMPERIAL YARD

DEGRAVE SHORT & Cº LONDON

[109] MEASUREMENT INDICATOR. This interesting device can be found on the front wall of the city chambers, George Sq.

[110] FIGURATIVE PROGRAMME, former Athenaeum theatre, 179 Buchanan St. *William Kellock Brown.*

[111] ENGINEERING, stock exchange, 159 Buchanan St. *John Mossman.* This is one of five roundels with projecting busts representing branches of commerce; the others are science, art, building and mining. The building [see **92**], one of Glasgow's finest, has many other interesting sculptures and carvings.

[112] LAW-LORD KEYSTONE, Royal Faculty of Procurators, 12 Nelson Mandela Pl. *Alexander Handyside Ritchie.* There are fourteen keystones with the heads of distinguished law lords and legal worthies on the façade [see **93**].

[113] CLYDE CLOCK, Killermont St. *George Wyllie*. Commissioned by Radio Clyde to celebrate the station's twenty-five years of broadcasting and gifted to Glasgow.

[114] WINCHER'S STANCE, Buchanan St. bus station, 1995, *John Clinch*. Title of statue chosen by readers of the Glasgow newspaper, *Evening Times*.

[115] PEACOCK, Princes Sq, 48 Buchanan St. *Alan Dawson*. A magnificent art nouveau giant in aluminium and bronze.

[116] ALLEGORICAL FIGURE: *TRUTH*, 60 Buchanan St. In left hand, mirror; in right, blindfold.

[117] BUCK'S HEAD BUILDING, 63 Argyle St. 1863, *Alexander Thomson*. The first major design by 'Greek' Thomson: remarkable curvature on the corner section, iron frames with directly inserted windows. The name recalls the previous site occupant, the Buck's Head hotel.

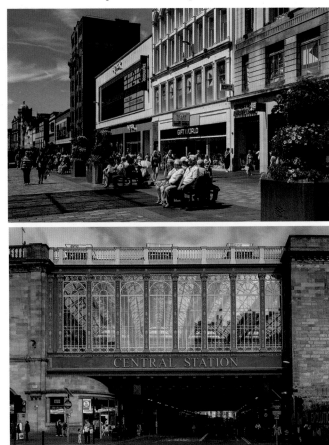

[118] ARGYLE STREET SHOPPING. This is Glasgow's busiest shopping street, with most of the major high-street chains represented, although it does not quite have the cachet of the adjoining Buchanan St.

[119] HIELANMAN'S UMBRELLA, Argyle St/ Central station viaduct, 1906, *James Miller*. The highly evocative nickname was coined because Scottish Highlanders who had come to Glasgow in search of work would congregate here at the weekends. Screens in cast-iron and glass.

[120] ARGYLL ARCADE INTERIOR, Argyle St. 1827, *John Baird*. Design influenced by London's Burlington arcade and now almost entirely given over to retailers specialising in jewellery, watches and clocks. The first shopping mall in Scotland [see **101**].

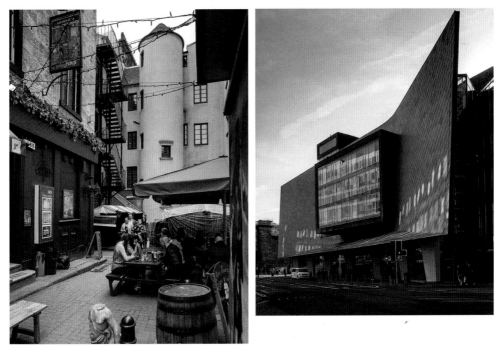

[121] SLOAN'S RESTAURANT, Argyll Arcade/Argyle St. Established in 1797, Sloan's is said to be the city's oldest restaurant and retains many period features. Couples would buy their engagement rings in the Argyll arcade and then celebrate in Sloan's. Wonderfully atmospheric bars, impressive grand ballroom.

[122] RADISSON BLU HOTEL, 301 Argyle St. 2002, *gm+ad*. The huge copper screen and the block of rooms that cantilever through it help to make this one of the most stylish buildings in Glasgow. Modern architecture at its best.

[123] ST ENOCH CENTRE, St Enoch Sq. 1989. With twenty million shoppers a year flocking to the dozens of stores, this is said to be the largest retail complex in Britain outside of London. Built on the site of several distinguished predecessors, including St Enoch station and its hotel, but the design fails to inspire.

[124] ST ENOCH UNDERGROUND STATION, St Enoch Sq. 1896, *James Miller*. A witty essay in Scottish baronial and Jacobean styles, indeed almost toy-like. The perfect antidote to the big shed behind it, this former underground station will charm anyone who cares to make its acquaintance.

[125] TEACHER'S BUILDING, 20 St Enoch Sq. 1875, *James Boucher*. Designed for William Teacher, whisky distillers, in the Italianate style. Four quite distinct floors with interesting carvings and cast-iron balconies.

[126] GARDNER AND SON WAREHOUSE, 36 Jamaica St. 1856, *John Baird*. Described by Pevsner as 'the most remarkable cast-iron warehouse of its date anywhere in Britain' and by another expert as 'one of the great landmarks of Western architectural history'. The apotheosis of Victorian ingenuity.

[127] STUDENT FLATS, Central House, 50–58 Jamaica St. A colourful, and contrasting, addition to the older buildings here.

[128] TOBACCO WAREHOUSE, 41–45 James Watt St. 1854, *John Baird*. The vast warehouses in this thoroughfare close to the Clyde speak to the scale of Glasgow's imports of food and tobacco during the nineteenth century. Some of the most important commercial buildings in the city are hereabouts.

[129] FORMER GLASGOW HERALD BUILDING, 60 Mitchell St. 1895, *Charles Rennie Mackintosh/ Honeyman & Keppie*. Now, quite appropriately, part of the Lighthouse, Scotland's centre for architecture and design. With elements of Scots baronial the corner site enabled the young Mackintosh to create the non-traditional and highly innovative 150-foot water tower.

[130] SPIRAL STAIRCASE, 60 Mitchell St, interior conversion *Page and Park*. *Mackintosh*'s water tower [see 129] is no less stunning from the inside, helped by the construction of a spiral staircase.

[131] EGYPTIAN HALLS, 84 Union St. 1873, *Alexander Thomson*. With similarities to his Grosvenor building in Gordon St. [see 142] this sophisticated and brilliantly executed design, over four very different storeys, brings together many of the ideas Thomson had previously explored. The eaves gallery, with its squat Egyptian columns, is a stroke of genius. Interior is framed in cast iron. Currently undergoing redevelopment and we can only hope that the decorative covers seen here are removed soon.

[132] HORSE SHOE BAR, 17 Drury St. 1870. The 104-foot island bar, in the shape of a horseshoe, is said to be the longest in Europe. This traditional pub is a Glasgow institution and the perfect place to recharge the batteries after a hard day's sightseeing.

[133]

[134]

[135]

[133] FORMER DAILY RECORD BUILDING, 20 Renfield Lane, 1901, *Charles Rennie Mackintosh*. A tall newspaper office ingeniously designed to be seen to best advantage in this narrow lane, with the white brick enhancing the limited opportunities for light.

[134] 13–17 RENFIELD ST. 1916, *James Miller*. The ground floor was once a lavish, 857-seat restaurant and tearoom owned by the legendary Miss Kate Cranston, of which, sadly, nothing now remains. Miller's tall Beaux Art building, however, can still be admired.

[135] PAVILION THEATRE, 121 Renfield St. 1904, *Bertie Crewe*. Opened as a music hall known as the Palace of Varieties, the Pavilion has remained true to its roots and to its patrons with a steady diet of panto, comedy, music and popular plays. Now styles itself as the Scottish National Theatre of Variety.

[136] CINEWORLD, 7 Renfrew St. 2001. Glasgow is a city of avid filmgoers and this mammoth complex with its eighteen screens spread over nine floors attracts nearly two million patrons a year, making it the busiest in Britain.

[137] HERALD/EVENING TIMES BUILDING, 200 Renfield St. The venerable *Herald* (formerly *Glasgow Herald*) is the oldest newspaper in the English-speaking world, dating back to 1783. Annan fountain of 1915 (*right*), commissioned by William Annan.

[138] RBS, 4–16 Gordon St. 1857, *David Rhind*. Described by Pevsner as 'one of Glasgow's finest palazzi'. The quality of the masonry, keystones and esp. the Italianate first-floor windows is exceptional [see **152**].

[139] GRAND CENTRAL HOTEL, Gordon St. 1884, *Sir Robert Rowand Anderson*. Perhaps the city's best-known hotel, guests have included JFK, Sir Winston Churchill and Frank Sinatra.

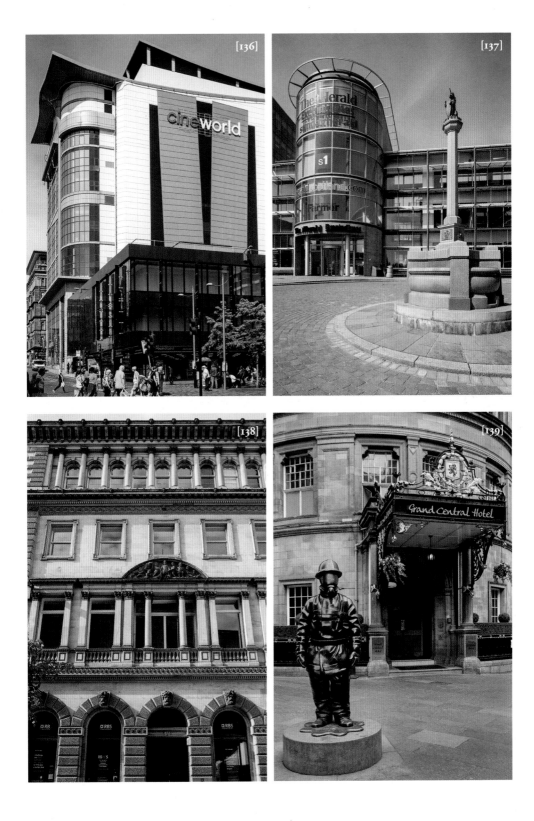

[140] CA' D'ORO, Gordon St/Union St. 1872, *John Honeyman*. This magnificent cast-iron palazzo is one of Glasgow's most distinctive and revered buildings. The name refers to the restaurant that operated here. [141] GORDON ST/HOPE ST. CORNER. The former Standard Life building (*left*) dates from 1890 and was designed by *James Thomson*. To the right sits the Grosvenor building. [142] GROSVENOR BUILDING, 72 Gordon St. 1859, *Alexander Thomson*. In close-up the superb detail of 'Greek' Thomson's warehouse is shown to best advantage.

[143] CENTRAL STATION, Gordon St. 1879, *Donald Matheson and others*. The city's most important railway station, with around thirty million passengers a year. It is a cathedral of rail with its huge glass roof, fifteen ground-level platforms and low-level departures below.

[144] 66–70 GORDON ST. 1902, *Sir J. J. Burnet*. This baroque pastiche replaced the Victorian warehouse here and was specially designed for Forsyth's, the city's leading outfitters, featuring mod cons like electric lifts and central heating. Interesting dome, carvings and statuary.

[145] GRAND CENTRAL HOTEL, from Hope St. 1884, *Sir Robert Rowand Anderson*. Originally conceived as offices, the owners changed their minds and ordered Anderson to create a hotel that would surpass the rival railway hotel at St Enoch station. Significant extension in early 20th c. by *James Miller*. Still one of the city's best known hotels, guests have included many world-famous actors, singers and politicians. The Swedish-style tower still dominates this locale.

[146]

[147]

[146] ATLANTIC CHAMBERS,
43 Hope St, 1899, *Sir J. J. Burnet*.
The best surviving example of
Burnet's modernism, bold and
simple, with eaves gallery, reflecting
American designs of the period.
Rear elevation in Cadogan St, with
its echoes of Chicago, also notable.

**[147] FORMER SCOTTISH
TEMPERANCE LEAGUE
BUILDING,** 106 Hope St. 1894,
Salmon & Gillespie. Franco-Flemish
in style. Quirky, yet refined, with
superb statuary and carvings, some
of them semi-naked figures,
perhaps not what we expect from
the Temperance movement!

**[148] LIVERPOOL AND
LONDON AND GLOBE
INSURANCE BUILDING,** Hope
St/St Vincent St. 1898, *J. B. & W. A.
Thomson*. This large, seven-storey
palazzo in red sandstone is one of
the most elaborate structures in the
city in a quarter replete with great
architecture. Rises impressively to a
dome and cupola. Superb sculpture.

[149] 157–167 HOPE ST. 1902, *John A. Campbell*. This eight-storey Spanish-style alcazar, with upper two-storey arcade – on the junction with W. George St. – is considered Campbell's masterpiece. Its massive size does not detract from the building's romantic appeal. Anderston-born, Campbell trained in Paris and was for a significant period a partner in the Burnet family's renowned architectural practice.

[150] THEATRE ROYAL, 282 Hope St. 1867, *George Bell*/1895, *Charles Phipps*. The western home of Scottish Opera since the Seventies it also stages music and dance from a range of genres. Rebuilt in 1895 by theatre architect par excellence Phipps after a fire. Interior was remodelled in 1975 following Phipps's style and is both sumptuous and elegant.

[151] ATLANTES, 134 Argyle St. 1903, *William Vickers*. One of a pair, muscular *Atlantes* is a highly appropriate ornament on a building that in its day was said to be one of the largest warehouses in Britain.

[152] CHERUBS WORKING PRINTING PRESS, 4–16 Gordon St. 1857, *John Thomas/Alexander Handyside Ritchie*. This allegorical relief is relatively unusual in the city, representing children doing adult work. It is a fine adornment to one of the most impressive commercial buildings in Glasgow [see **138**].

[153] COLUMBIA AND BRITANNIA, 43 Hope St. 1899, *McGilvray & Ferris*. The transatlantic theme of *Burnet*'s Atlantic chambers [see **146**] is reflected in these red-sandstone carvings. *Columbia*'s shield adorned with stars and stripes.

[154] ABSTRACT, 60 Mitchell St. *Charles Rennie Mackintosh*. A typically stylish flourish by the young CRM [see **129**].

Glasgow's Art

In 1990 Glasgow was designated European Capital of Culture, following in the distinguished footsteps of Athens, Florence, Amsterdam, Berlin and Paris. It was the culmination of years of hard work by the city to reshape its image, for example through the successful Glasgow's Miles Better campaign of 1983.

Glasgow's artistic roots go back centuries. In 1754 the Foulis Academy of Fine Arts was set up by Robert Foulis, fifteen years before the opening of the Royal Academy. As the city's wealth grew the business elite amassed fine collections, most notably Archibald McLellan (1796–1854), who left his art to the city. Glasgow University was also prominent: in 1807 the Hunterian, Scotland's first public museum, opened on High Street thanks to funding provided by 'father of anatomy' William Hunter (1718–83).

The serious collecting continued. To complement his fine mansion, Pollok House, William Stirling Maxwell (1818–78) filled its rooms with art. His greatest passion was for Spanish paintings and works by Goya and El Greco adorn the walls; the most admired being the latter's *Lady in a Fur Wrap* (*see facing page*). If the Maxwell family had a successor it was shipping magnate Sir William Burrell. After selling his business in 1916 Burrell focused on his art collection, which grew exponentially. In 1944 he assigned it to the city of his birth, and, in 1963, a decision was made to provide a purpose-built facility for the collection in Pollok Park. Known as the Burrell collection, it was opened by the Queen in 1983. On display are works by Degas, Renoir, Manet, Pissarro, Whistler and Rodin, to name but a few.

Glasgow City Council is custodian of the finest municipal art collection in Britain. The vast majority of its pieces are located in Kelvingrove art gallery, a 1901 behemoth. Kelvingrove's range is impressive: from arms and armour to artefacts from ancient Egypt, although it is also renowned for its Old Master paintings. The most popular piece however is from a different era: *Christ of St John of the Cross* (*see below*) by the great surrealist Salvador Dali. Painted in 1951 and purchased by the city for just £8,000, in 1952, it is now valued at around £60 million.

Glasgow has produced many talented artists. The Glasgow School, or the Glasgow Boys, was an informal grouping of twenty artists – including E. A. Hornel, Sir John Lavery and James Guthrie – who reacted against the stultifying conventions of Victorian painting. There are

William Stirling Maxwell

El Greco, *Lady in a Fur Wrap*

extensive holdings of the Boys' works, both at Kelvingrove and in the Hunterian art gallery.

The role of the Glasgow School of Art cannot be underestimated. The influential Glasgow Style was developed by a small group of its students, 'The Four': Charles Rennie Mackintosh, his wife Margaret MacDonald, Margaret's sister, Frances Macdonald, and Herbert MacNair. The apotheosis of the Glasgow Style is Margaret MacDonald's 1902 art nouveau masterpiece, *The Heart of the Rose*, which appears below. GSA alumni have continued to be highly influential: Benno Schotz in sculpture, Joan Eardley in painting, Jack Coia in architecture, Oscar Marzaroli in photography, Alasdair Gray in writing, Robbie Coltrane and Peter Capaldi in acting. Then there is the prestigious Turner Prize, won for three years in a row by GSA alumni: Richard Wright (2009), Susan Philipsz (2010) and Martin Boyce (2011).

The city's place in the rarefied world of the fine arts seems assured.

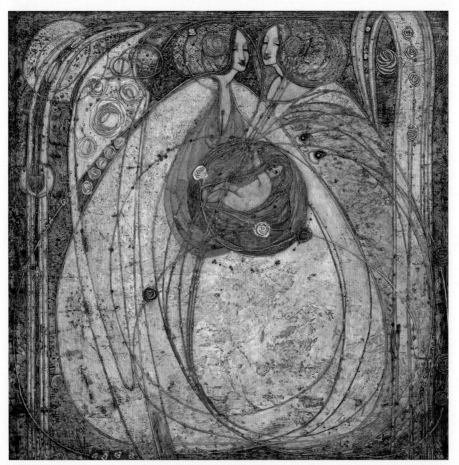

Margaret MacDonald, *The Heart of the Rose*

Salvador Dali, *Christ of St John of the Cross*

[155] DISTILLER'S BUILDING, 64 Waterloo St. 1900, *James Chalmers*. Built for distillers Wright and Greig. Conventional façade on the west side but highly idiosyncratic on the east side with strange 'barley-sugar' columns on the tower. One of the statues above the entrance is of the Sir Walter Scott (*Lady of the Lake*) character Roderick Dhu, which was the name of the company's most famous whisky and was produced at the Dallas Dhu distillery near Forres.

[156] WATERLOO CHAMBERS,
15 Waterloo St. 1900, *Sir J. J. Burnet*.
Although larger, this complex, American-
elevator design resembles Burnet's Atlantic
chambers round the corner in Hope St
[see **146**]. He intended to make it two
storeys higher but fire regulations got in
the way. Its tall, vertical façade includes
Ionic columns and rich carvings.

[157] SENTINEL BUILDING, 103
Waterloo St. 2004, *gm+ad*. Multi-award-
winning building designed by a local firm.
Located in the heart of the city's financial-
services district, its ten floors provide
85,000 square feet of office space and the
specially designed lighting system produces
a spectacular display. One of many fine
modern designs in this part of the city.

[158] FORMER ROYAL BANK
BUILDING, 30 Bothwell St. 1935, *James
Miller*. This tall, white cube is a stark
contrast to the 19th c. structures to either
side and the Greek details with classical
frieze (by *Gilbert Bayes*) represent another
break with Miller's baroque designs of the
pre-1914 period.

[156]

[157]

[158]

[159] SCOTTISH LEGAL ASSURANCE SOCIETY BUILDING, 81 Bothwell St. 1927, *Wylie, Wright & Wylie*. A behemoth, yet elegant and dignified, this American-style competition winner, which occupies an entire block, is surely one of the most impressive commercial buildings in Scotland. Fine carvings and reliefs adorn the façade.

[160] AURORA BUILDING, 120 Bothwell St. 2007, *Cooper Cromar*. Another fine modern building in the heart of the commercial centre, again designed by a local firm. Ten storeys with huge, open-plan floors providing flexible office accommodation. The curved façade is particularly noteworthy.

[161] FORMER CENTRAL THREAD AGENCY, 36–62 Bothwell St. 1900, *H. & D. Barclay*. A tall, baroque, Franco-Flemish extravagance built for the well-known firm of J. & P. Coats, thread manufacturers. Richly decorated, with a rather crowded façade.

[162] FORMER CENTRAL THREAD AGENCY. This close-up shows the Barclay design in greater detail.

[161]

[160]

[162]

[163] BANK OF SCOTLAND, 110–120 St Vincent St. 1927, *James Miller*. Inspired by Hislop's bank at no. 78 [see **164**] and two bank buildings in New York, Miller's superb design would not look out of place in either the Big Apple or Chicago. Monumental in scale the towering Ionic columns and double-height windows dwarf the passer-by and help make this one of the most imposing commercial buildings in Glasgow.

[164] PAPERINO'S, 78 St Vincent St. 1913, *A. D. Hislop*. Originally the Phoenix Assurance building, later the Bank of Credit and Commerce and now a restaurant. Glasgow's first American-style design, one that proved highly influential in the interwar years. Interesting Doric columns, which contrast nicely with the granite upper floors. As one commentator notes: 'Edwardian exuberance is out and a monumental neo-classicism is in'.

[167]

[166]

[165] HATRACK BUILDING (detail), 144 St Vincent St. 1902, *James Salmon II*. One of Glasgow's great architectural feats, cramming ten storeys onto a plot less than thirty feet wide. Front wall almost wholly of glass with art nouveau detailing. The projecting finials on the top floor, shown here, give the building its 'Hatrack' nickname. **[166]** HATRACK BUILDING, (façade).

[167] NORWICH UNION CHAMBERS, 125 St Vincent St. 1898, *John Hutchison*. Northern Renaissance design rising to a conical roof tower. One of several eye-catching commercial buildings in the St Vincent St/Hope St. section.

[168] ST VINCENT STREET CHURCH, 265 St Vincent St. 1859, *Alexander Thomson.* Built for the United Presbyterians, this is one of the great European churches and a living testament to 'Greek' Thomson's genius. Said to have Solomon's temple as its inspiration, it is raised on a huge podium containing halls and other apartments. Original ideas abound: the massive plinth; the unorthodox, asymmetric tower; the Egyptian, Greek and Roman motifs.

St Vincent Street Church

[169] THE TOWER. The superb detailing of the tower is seen to best effect in close-up.

[170] WINDOW AND CLASSICAL FIGURES. This church is the most elaborately ornamented in Thomson's oeuvre.

[171] INTERIOR. The rich colours one finds on the inside are a stark contrast to the rather austere exterior. The platform is particularly satisfying with its distinct symmetry, into which Thomson has fitted each element to perfection, from the long pulpit to the organ.

[172] 151 ST VINCENT STREET. With its seventy thousand square feet of office space, this striking edifice in copper, glass and granite compares favourably to the Victorian and Edwardian palazzi that grace the city's commercial hub.

[173] 200 ST VINCENT STREET, 1929, *Sir J. J. Burnet.* Simple yet masterful this Italianate design was Burnet's last in Glasgow. Figures over the entrance, added later, are superb. Glasgow-born Burnet was one of the city's greatest architects, honoured with the gold medal of the Paris Salon and a knighthood for his design of the King Edward VII galleries in the British Museum.

[174] ROYAL COLLEGE OF PHYSICIANS AND SURGEONS OF GLASGOW, 242 St Vincent St. 1830s, remodelled by *Sir J. J. Burnet*. The college was founded in 1599 with the grant of a charter from King James VI, moving here in 1862, and now has ten thousand members. Building originally a private house, imaginatively altered by Burnet in 1893.

[175] HILTON HOTEL, 1 William St. Towering over its competitor, the nearby Marriott, the Hilton affords superb views of the city and much beyond.

[176] CONNAL'S BUILDING, 34 W. George St. 1900, *James Thomson*. The Connals were warehouse-keepers but this six-storey sandstone extravagance is far from utilitarian. Modelled on the Ritter inn, Heidelberg, with onion corner dome. Heads, carved by *James Young*, represent well-known Glasgow entrepreneurs like Watt, Dixon, Baird and Connell himself.

[177] JAMES SELLARS HOUSE, 144 W. George St. 1881, *James Sellars*. Formerly the New Club, but renamed for the architect in 1981. Shows not only the influence of the French Second Empire with its oval windows and cast-iron balconies but also of Alexander 'Greek' Thomson in the bands of windows. Regrettably, behind the façade, we find only the remodelling of the late 1970s.

[178] 92 WEST GEORGE STREET, 1937, *James Miller*. Built for the Commercial Bank the simple, American-style design in white Portland stone is highly effective and nicely complemented by the decorative wall panels. Now a restaurant. Miller (1860–1947) left a considerable imprint on Glasgow with designs for a wide variety of buildings [see 158 and 163] and on Scotland generally with, for example, his luxury Ayrshire hotel, Turnberry.

[179] 117 WEST GEORGE STREET, 1894, *William Leiper*. A superb French Renaissance essay that fittingly won a silver medal at the 1900 Paris Exhibition. Fine sculpture by *William Birnie Rhind* including, high up on the Renfield St. side, copies of three of Michelangelo's masterpieces: *David* and two figures from the Medici chapel in Florence.

[180] 196 WEST GEORGE STREET, 1820s. This elegant, symmetrical five-bay house, with pediment and stairs, is perhaps the finest survivor of the Blythswood New Town of the early 19th c. [see 189–190]. Glasgow was moving west in a big way and the new development on Blythswood Hill symbolised the change. Note the central chimney-stalk with its scrolls and fluted pots.

[181] WEST GEORGE STREET, looking east. This view features some interesting buildings, including (*left*) the thirteen-storey, modernist bulk of the former Glasgow College of Building and Printing (now part of City of Glasgow College) and (*middle*) St George's Tron. The street, the western extension of George St. is named after King George III, as of course is George Square.

[182] MALMAISON HOTEL, 278 W. George St. 1839, *John Stephen*. The former St Jude's, a Scottish Episcopal church, designed in the Greek Revival style. It is now a hotel. Sadly, the replica of the Monument of Lysicrates (near the Athens Acropolis), which adorned the main porch, shown here, was taken down in the 1960s.

[183] VICTORIA BUILDINGS, 2–4 W. Regent St. 1860, *Jonathan Bell*. Pevsner sums up these business chambers perfectly: 'English Tudor meets Scottish castellated' and they do provide a real contrast with other city-centre designs of the Victorian period. Eastern section demolished in 1974 to make way for Standard Life House.

[184] PRUDENTIAL BUILDING, W. Regent St/Renfield St. 1890, *Paul Waterhouse*. Thomas De Quincey, essayist and author of *Confessions of an English Opium Eater*, lived here. An eclectic mix of Scottish baronial and Flemish forms. Ground-floor restaurant, which occupies the former tellers' room, has wonderful period tiled walls.

[185] CASTLE CHAMBERS, W. Regent St/Renfield St. 1902, *James Carruthers*. Sumptuous eight-storey pile in red sandstone built for the brewers and distillers, Maclachlan and Co, owners of the Castle brewery in Maryhill and the Auchentoshan distillery. They ran a restaurant on the ground floor here; hence the large plate-glass windows. Pre-Raphaelite maidens in brackets [see **237**]. The Maclachlan brothers also owned a number of pubs in Glasgow, which they kept well-stocked with their Castle pale ales and stouts.

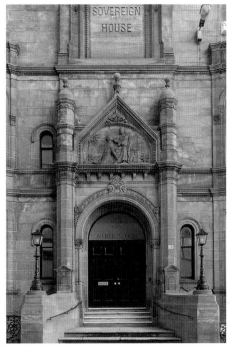

[186] FORMER JOHN ROSS MEMORIAL CHURCH FOR THE DEAF, 160 W. Regent St. 1931, *Norman Dick*. The church, in red sandstone, is cleverly linked to the adjoining former Institute for the Adult Deaf and Dumb at no. 158 [see **187** and **188**].

[187] SOVEREIGN HOUSE, 158 W. Regent St. 1894, *Robert Duncan*. A former institute for the deaf and dumb, now offices, in an Arts and Crafts style. Interesting details including, over the door: **[188]** CHRIST HEALING THE DEAF AND DUMB MAN, a scene from St Mark's Gospel, set in the Holy Land and describing the return of Jesus to the Sea of Galilee. Complete with palm trees and domed building, we see the deaf and dumb man being healed by Jesus. The word *ephphatha* is Greek for 'be opened'.

[189] BLYTHSWOOD HOTEL, 11 Blythswood Sq. 1820s, *John Brash*. Blythswood Sq, on Blythswood Hill, was part of a large estate owned by the Campbells of Blythswood, one of the city's richest families, who sold it off in parcels to enterprising developers. The building shown here was part of one such development and was at the centre of Glasgow's second new town, known as Blythswood. Now a hotel – it was formerly the Royal Scottish Automobile Club – it is one of four elegant classical terraces facing a central garden.

[190] LADY ARTISTS' CLUB, 5 Blythswood Sq. [details as for **189**]. Notable for the remarkable entrance door, 1908, by Charles Rennie Mackintosh and for his and George Walton's remodelling of the interior. Next door, no. 7, was the home of socialite Madeleine Smith, tried in 1857 for the murder, by arsenic poisoning, of her lover Pierre L'Angelier. It is Glasgow's most celebrated crime, helped by the not-proven verdict that electrified the city.

[191] SPECTRUM BUILDING, 55 Blythswood St. *gm+ad*. Imaginative, witty and irreverent refurbishment of a 1960s office block. The use of shiny stainless-steel cladding has led, inevitably, to it being nicknamed the Turkey-in-Bacofoil or Kit Kat building.

[192] 127–129 BATH ST. 1910, *H. E. Clifford*. Redesigned as education offices by Clifford, now a hotel. Giant Ionic columns above hooded entrance. As the small wall plaque notes, also the early home of Glasgow-born Sir Henry Campbell-Bannerman, the former MP for Stirling Burghs and Liberal prime minister, who occupied 10 Downing St. from 1905–8.

[193] ADELAIDE PLACE BAPTIST CHURCH, 209 Bath St. 1877, *T. L. Watson*. The Baptist congregation has worshipped in this city-centre location continuously since 1877 and continues to make an important contribution to the local community. Striking design with windows, pediment and Corinthian columns influenced by 'Greek' Thomson.

[194] FORMER GLASGOW ACADEMY,
8 Elmbank St. 1847, *Charles Wilson*. The great
architect's first iteration of his Italianate style. The
magnificent *John Mossman* figures on the plinths are
of Homer, Galileo, Watt and Cicero. Later occupied
by Glasgow High School; today council offices. Much
extended since Wilson's day.

[195] RENFIELD ST STEPHEN, 260 Bath St. 1852,
J. T. Emmett. First example of Tractarian Gothic in
Glasgow, with breathtaking tall spire and fine
stained-glass windows. Saved from demolition in the
late 1960s but badly affected by the unnecessary
removal of sculpture when the modern extension to
the west was built.

[196] KING'S THEATRE, 297 Bath St. 1904, *Frank
Matcham*. Steady stream of musicals and comedy but
renowned for its Christmas pantos, which have
starred Scottish showbiz legends like Stanley Baxter,
Jimmy Logan and Rikki Fulton. Typically brilliant
design by Matcham, the theatre architect nonpareil,
who was also responsible for the London Palladium.

[197] SAVOY CENTRE, 128–152 Sauchiehall St. 1893, *H. & D. Barclay*. This former furniture warehouse, now a shopping arcade, has a spectacular façade with Ionic columns, carvings and allegorical figures, the latter attributed to *William Birnie Rhind*. Described by Pevsner as a 'feast for the eyes'.

[198] GRECIAN CHAMBERS, 336–356 Sauchiehall St. 1865, *Alexander Thomson*. Modest in scale at three storeys but a highly inventive design, the highlight being the squat Egyptian columns on the top

floor, which appear to stand free from the glazing; this was a quite revolutionary concept for the time. A piece of trivia for architecture lovers: this is the only place where the designs of 'Greek' Thomson and Charles Rennie Mackintosh (Glasgow School of Art, *right*) can be seen together, as **198a** shows.

[199] WILLOW TEA ROOMS, 217 Sauchiehall St. 1904, *Charles Rennie Mackintosh*. The last tearoom designed by Mackintosh for Miss Cranston and the only one that was a complete building both inside and out. The floor above the sign has a stunning decorative and leaded bow window and indicates the position of the fabled Room de Luxe, now painstakingly restored and once again in use a tearoom.

[200] BANK OF SCOTLAND, 235 Sauchiehall St. 1931, *A. Graham Henderson*. A somewhat plain, yet pleasing, box this is one of the few buildings of merit on this stretch. Enhanced by some marvellous sculpture by *Benno Schotz* the interior is also worthy of note.

[201] MCLELLAN GALLERIES/ TRERON BUILDING, 254–290 Sauchiehall St. 1856, *James Smith*. Built to house the art collection of Archibald McLellan, a wealthy Glasgow merchant and keen patron of the visual arts. The building also served as the opulent Tréron et Cie department store. Currently empty but with plans to reopen.

[202] BERESFORD BUILDING, 460 Sauchiehall St. 1938, *Weddell & Inglis*. This ten-storey art deco structure, a true Glasgow landmark, was originally the Beresford hotel, its first task being to accommodate visitors to the 1938 Empire Exhibition. Later sold to ICI for its Scottish HQ before becoming Baird hall, a student residence; now private apartments.

[203–204] CHARING CROSS. One of the city's most elegant and historic locales, linking the city centre – at the foot of Sauchiehall St. – with the west end. Unfortunately, the immediate area was ripped apart to make way for the M8 motorway, although at least *Sir J. J. Burnet*'s magnificent Charing Cross mansions of 1891 [203, *above right*] survived. On the façade the spectacular Francophile curves of Burnet's exuberant design are enhanced by the grand bronze clock with its roman numerals and sculptor *William Birnie Rhind*'s *Figurative Programme*, featuring male and female figures.

[205–210] GLASGOW SCHOOL OF ART, 167 Renfrew St. 1899 and 1909, *Charles Rennie Mackintosh*. When the school's distinguished director, Fra Newbery, drew up the requirements for a new building his specifications were exacting and precise. Glasgow-born Charles Rennie Mackintosh, a GSA alumnus, met the challenge head-on and his competition entry brilliantly fulfilled Newbery's strict criteria. Despite the hilly and restricted site Mackintosh was able to fashion a building that many consider the city's crowning glory, one that continues to entrance both Glaswegians and visitors. The art school must be considered his masterpiece and is without doubt one of the most influential works of twentieth-century architecture. The eclecticism is marked, ranging from the brilliant art nouveau touches of the main entrance [205 and 205a] to the Scottish vernacular of the east façade [206] and the later west façade with its experimental, modernist look [207]. The interior is equally innovative and the pièce de résistance for many is the wonderful double-height galleried library [208], which, with its dark timber has a distinct Japanese sensibility, evoking a forest. Badly damaged by fire in May 2014.

[209] KEYSTONE RELIEF. Mackintosh and his fellow members in artistic group 'The Four' (his wife Margaret Macdonald was a member, an influential designer in her own right) had a strong affinity with the mystical Rosicrucian movement, which held that the rose was *the* symbol of nature. This fascinating art nouveau piece on the exterior of the GSA epitomises that philosophy. [210] In this quirky finial, Mackintosh essays a degree of verisimilitude with the Glasgow coat of arms.

[211] REID BUILDING, Glasgow School of Art, Renfrew St. 2014, *Steven Holl*. Given its very close proximity to Mackintosh's original GSA, Holl's glass-and-concrete extension – which incorporates the stone assembly building – was always likely to be closely scrutinised. It is fair to say that critical reaction was mixed although the interiors have been praised in some quarters for the way in which natural light is maximised.

[212] ROYAL CONSERVATOIRE OF SCOTLAND, 100 Renfrew St. 1988, *Sir Leslie Martin with Ivor Richards*. With its brick colonnades and quiet classicism this design by Martin, who was also responsible for the Royal Concert Hall, divided opinion.

[213] GLASGOW DENTAL HOSPITAL AND SCHOOL, 203 Renfrew St. 1931, *Wylie, Wright & Wylie*. While there is a large modern extension facing Sauchiehall St. this is by far the more interesting side, with its cast-iron panels and art deco flourishes. The dental campus is part of the school of medicine of Glasgow University and offers a range of undergraduate and postgraduate degrees.

[214] GARNETHILL GARDENS, Hill St/Rose St. A charming, offbeat little park that has come to symbolise the regeneration of the bohemian Garnethill neighbourhood, home to so many fine cultural institutions. Local residents provided the quotes for the concrete slabs, which give fascinating insights into the area's history.

[215] GLASGOW FILM THEATRE, 12 Rose St. 1939, *W. J. Anderson II*. The Cosmo, as it was originally known, was the first purpose-built, art-house cinema outside of London. Seventy-five years on it is still bringing the cream of world film to discerning patrons on its three screens. Distinctive design, with stepped tower, based on the Curzon cinema, Mayfair; impressive art deco interiors.

[216] ST ALOYSIUS COLLEGE, 45 Hill St. 1883, *Archibald Macpherson*. The city's leading Catholic school is run by the Society of Jesus, or Jesuits, and has around 1,250 pupils in its kindergarten, primary and secondary divisions. A Venetian palazzo with Doric portico. Built on the site of the former Collegiate school.

[217]

[218]

ST ALOYSIUS, 25 Rose St. 1910, *C. J. Menart*. [217] Jesuit Catholic church. Exterior Roman Renaissance but in red sandstone with tall tower and domed bell-stage. [218] Lavish interior includes four side chapels, a shrine to St John Ogilvie (a Jesuit martyr hanged at Glasgow Cross in 1615 and Scotland's first saint for 700 years) and magnificent marbled high altar based on shrine of St Aloysius in S. Ignazio, Rome. [219] The dome features Jesuit saints including Ignatius of Loyola, founder of that order.

[220] BREADALBANE TERRACE, Hill St. 1846, *possibly Charles Wilson.* Like Peel Tce. opposite **[221]**, but perhaps more exuberant, this is one of Glasgow's finest tenement blocks. Square-columned Doric porches, decorated first-floor pediments and balustrade parapets.

[221] PEEL TERRACE, Hill St. 1842, *possibly Charles Wilson.* An attractive four-storey Georgian terrace with eighteen bays consisting of main-door houses and common-stair flats. Alternating pediments over first-floor windows. On the crest of the hill, which shows the terrace off to best advantage.

[222] GARNETHILL SYNAGOGUE,
129 Hill St. 1879, *John McLeod with Nathan
Solomon Joseph*. Opened by the Glasgow
Hebrew Congregation, this is Scotland's first
purpose-built synagogue and the most-
important place of worship for the country's
Jewish community. Designed for an orthodox
congregation, in which women traditionally
sat upstairs in the ladies' gallery. McLeod's
A-listed design is a mixture of Romanesque,
Byzantine and Gothic elements and is
considered one of the finest synagogues in
Europe. Stunning and much-visited interior.

[223] TENEMENT HOUSE, 145 Buccleuch St.
1892. Run by the National Trust for Scotland,
this is a perfectly preserved four-room house
that reveals Glasgow life in the first half of the
twentieth century. Miss Agnes Toward, a
shorthand typist, lived here from 1911–65 and
many of her possessions are on display.

[224] FORMER GARNETHILL PUBLIC
SCHOOL, 83 Buccleuch St. 1878, *James
Thomson*. An impressive-looking, council-
owned institution designed in the Italianate
style, with large central tower. From the outset
it was a centre of educational excellence and in
1894 became the Glasgow High School for
Girls, which was said to be the biggest
exclusively female school in Scotland. Now
residential flats.

[225] RODERICK DHU, 64 Waterloo St. 1900, *Richard Ferris*. One of a number of characters from Scott's epic poem *Lady of the Lake* represented on this building [see **155**].

[226] MERCURY and [227] INDUSTRY, both 35–69 Bothwell St. 1898, *Francis Derwent Wood*. Some fine sculpture adorns *Salmon & Gillespie*'s Mercantile chambers, including the seated *Mercury* and an allegorical *Industry*, who is holding a distaff.

[228] THRIFT and [229] ROYAL ARMS OF SCOTLAND, both 81 Bothwell St. 1931, *Archibald Dawson & James A. Young*. The huge, yet impressive, insurance company office block [see **159**] is perfectly complemented by its stylish art deco panels, which include *Thrift*. The large coat of arms, the *Royal Arms of Scotland*, is a nice patriotic touch and, in its own way, equally admirable.

[230] ST ANDREW, 200 St Vincent St. c. 1930, *Archibald Dawson*. The superb figures here, including St Andrew, beautifully set off *Sir J. J. Burnet*'s simple yet elegant palazzo [see **173**].

[231] INDUSTRIAL SCENE, [232] WILLIAM CONNAL both 34 W. George St. *James Young*. The idiosyncratic sculptural ornamentation here, known as Connal's building [see **176**], is well worth close inspection.

[233] OVAL WINDOW and [234] FRIEZE, 144 W. George St. 1881, *James Sellars/William Mossman*. More than a whiff of the French Second Empire in this window, the frieze and in other details on James Sellars House [see **177**].

[235] ESCUTCHEON WITH MARITIME SCENE, Ocean chambers, 188 W. George St. 1901, *unknown sculptor*. The original owners were in maritime insurance, hence the evocative imagery of lighthouse, galleons and walruses.

[236] ST JOHN THE BAPTIST, 98 W. Regent St. 1896, *unknown sculptor*. Building was commissioned by Lodge of St John, Glasgow, and so this wonderful figure and other carvings here are replete with Masonic symbolism.

[237] ALLEGORICAL FEMALE FIGURES, W. Regent St/Renfield St. 1902, *William Kellock Brown*. These wonderful Pre-Raphaelite maidens are at ground level in recessed compartments on this former brewer's building [see **185**].

[238] ALLEGORICAL FIGURES, Savoy centre, 128 Sauchiehall St. 1894, *William Birnie Rhind*. The figures are holding a galleon and a torch; on the right, a smiling sun [see **197**].

[239]

[239] ALLEGORICAL FIGURES,
235 Sauchiehall St. 1931, *Benno Schotz*.
The female figure (*left*) stands on a bracket
featuring a lion rampant while the male
(*right*) is atop a saltire. Fine adornments to Henderson's austere bank
[see **200**].

[240] ST MUNGO, Renfrew St. *Unknown*. The patron saint of Glasgow;
rear of McLellan galleries.

[241] JOHN STEWART, 121 Douglas St. 1921, *William Kellock Brown*.
Stewart was the founder of the City of Glasgow Friendly Society and
in this life-size bronze he is shown teaching a barefoot boy to read.

[242] DELPHIC SYBIL AND PROPHET ISAIAH, 518 Sauchiehall St.
1904, *McGilvray & Ferris*. *Charles Rennie Mackintosh* produced the
drawings for this building, which was designed for the eminent
photographic firm of T. & R. Annan & Sons. CRM's admiration for the
Sistine chapel evident in the Michelangelesque figures.

[242]

[243] ST ANDREW'S SUSPENSION BRIDGE, 1856, engineer *Neil Robson*. Sometimes called Harvey's bridge after Bailie Harvey, who was responsible for its erection. The wrought-iron structure was a safer river crossing for workers heading for the mills and factories of Calton and Bridgeton. Before the bridge they were reliant on a ferry.

[244] ROWERS ON THE CLYDE. The view from the suspension bridge [see **243**]. It is gratifying that Glasgow's great river is being enjoyed by its people for recreational purposes. In fact, rowing on the Clyde has been a popular pastime for a century or more, with one club tracing its roots back to mid-Victorian times. Historic west boathouse on north bank (*not shown here*).

[245] TIDAL WEIR BRIDGE, 1901 rebuilt 1949, *Robert Bruce*. Steel structure, with piers and abutments of red sandstone. The bridge also carries large-diameter pipes across the river. The main purpose of the weir is to maintain upstream water levels for environmental and recreational use.

[246] ALBERT BRIDGE, 1871, *R. Bell & D. Miller*. There have been five bridges at the end of Saltmarket including one designed by Robert Stevenson, grandfather of Robert Louis Stevenson. Said to be one of the most ambitious cast-iron bridges ever constructed. The cast-iron spandrels bear the coats of arms of Prince Albert, the royal family, various corporate bodies and Glasgow.

[247] GLASGOW COLLEGE OF NAUTICAL STUDIES, 21 Thistle St. 1969, *unknown*. Students training for the merchant navy study here, a constituent part of City of Glasgow College. The Gateway building was opened in 2004.

[248] VICTORIA BRIDGE, 1854, *James Walker*. Connecting Clyde St. and Gorbals St. this is Glasgow's oldest surviving bridge over the Clyde. At the time of construction was one of the two widest in Britain. Replaced Bishop Rae's bridge of c. 1350, which for four hundred years was the only permanent Clyde crossing. Five superb granite arches.

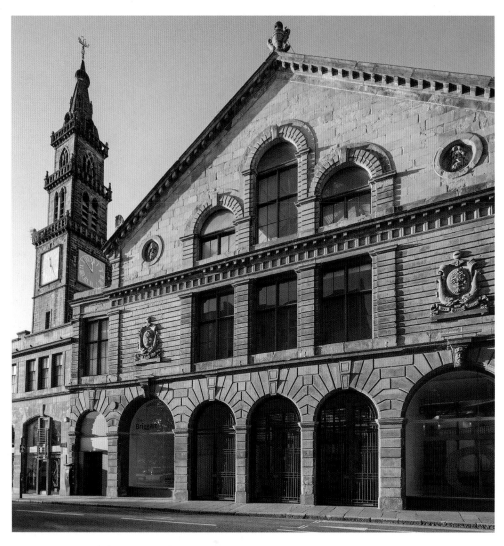

BRIGGAIT, 64 Clyde St. 1873, *Clarke & Bell*. [249] (*Bridgegate façade*) Served as Glasgow's fish market for a hundred years. Later extension incorporated Merchants' steeple (*left*) of 1665, which, with its delightful mix of Renaissance and Gothic styles, was a highly sophisticated design for the time. The steeple is all that is left of the Merchants' hall, which was built six years earlier in 1659. [250] (*Clyde St. façade*) Superb Second Empire detailing dominated by two columned gateways. [251] The refurbished interior, now an arts-and-craft centre, has beautiful cast-iron galleries with a glazed roof providing abundant natural light. A delight.

[252] WINGED SEAHORSES AND QUEEN VICTORIA PORTRAIT, 64 Clyde St. 1873, *not known*. The columned gateways of the Briggait [see 250] are topped off with these distinctive winged sea horses and the fine portraits of Victoria.

[253] LAURIESTON HOUSE, 52 Carlton Pl. 1802, *Peter Nicholson*. A superb terrace facing the Clyde and set off perfectly by the pedimented centre, in which the Laurie brothers, property developers, had their mansions. Their intention was to create an elegant suburb, Laurieston, but the rapid growth of Glasgow's industries put paid to their dream.

[254] SOUTH PORTLAND STREET SUSPENSION BRIDGE, 1853, *George Martin/ Alexander Kirkland*. A fine cast-iron and sandstone footbridge. Although it has been substantially rebuilt several times the Grecian-style triumphal arches are the originals and are therefore the oldest surviving elements on any Clyde crossing.

ST ANDREW'S CATHEDRAL,
170 Clyde St. 1816, *James Gillespie Graham*.

[255] The growth of Glasgow's Irish Catholic population in the late 18th c. led Father Andrew Scott to promote a new church, which cost £16,000 to build, an astronomical sum for the time. The Scottish RC hierarchy was restored in 1878 and in 1884 St Andrew's, a Gothic Revival design, was designated a cathedral.

[256] Renowned ecclesiastical architects *Pugin & Pugin* (sons of the great Augustus Pugin, the designer responsible for the Houses of Parliament) refurbished the interior in the 1880s and 1890s, bringing it up to cathedral standard. Further renovations, completed in 2011, give it a light-filled, colourful ambience.

[257] The cathedral's cloister garden – which has its own discrete entrance on Clyde St. – is an oasis of calm in a busy city. The garden has a number of mirrored plinths telling the story of the cathedral and the archdiocese of Glasgow.

[258] CUSTOM HOUSE, 298 Clyde St. 1840, *John Taylor*. A relatively modest structure given Glasgow's importance as a 19th c. trading centre. Greek Doric design and perhaps most notable for the splendid coat of arms on the roof.

[259] LA PASIONARIA, Clyde St. 1979, *Arthur Dooley*. Dolores Ibarruri (1895–1989) was a communist from the Basque country who played a prominent role on the Republican side in the Spanish civil war. 'La Pasionaria' (the passion flower), as she became known, was a great orator and propagandist who coined the phrase, 'Better to die on your feet than to live forever on your knees.' Unlike many of her comrades she survived the civil war and after General Franco's death was elected to the Cortes, Spain's parliament.

BETTER TO DIE ON YOUR FEET THAN
LIVE FOR EVER ON YOUR KNEES – Dolores Ibarruri
(La Pasionaria)

[260] GLASGOW (OR JAMAICA STREET) BRIDGE, 1899, *Blyth & Westland*. Replaced a bridge designed by the great Scottish engineer and architect, Thomas Telford. Although larger than that crossing, the seven spans match Telford's original.

[261] BANK OF SCOTLAND, Carlton Pl/Bridge St. 1857, *John Burnet*. Interesting corner building with two classical figures holding the bank's coat of arms.

[262] CALEDONIAN RAILWAY BRIDGES, 1905. The first bridge was built in 1878 (engineer *B. H. Blyth*) but today only the piers, seen here in the foreground, remain intact. The second bridge (engineer *Donald Matheson*) dates from 1905 and was required due to the expansion of Central station and carries up to ten tracks.

[263] KING GEORGE V BRIDGE, 1928, *Considère Constructions Ltd*. Three-arch structure of reinforced concrete covered with a facing of granite masonry. Links Commerce and Oswald streets.

[264] TRADESTON FOOTBRIDGE, 2009, *Halcrow*. Steel frame with concrete piers; sinuous curves, hence the nickname 'Squiggly bridge'. The fins above the deck support the bridge and are not merely stylistic. Links up-and-coming Tradeston with the international financial-services quarter, which can be seen in the background.

[265] ATLANTIC QUAY, 2009. In the heart of the financial-services district, around 16,000 people are employed in Atlantic Quay's six huge office blocks. Perhaps symbolises Glasgow's gradual transition from industrial powerhouse to service-sector hub.

[266] BROOMIELAW. With a name deriving from Brumelaw Croft, a stretch of land on the Clyde's north bank, the Broomielaw was the site of the city's first quay, built in 1688. Later it became known to generations of Glaswegians as the embarkation point for 'doon-the-watter' ferry trips to the likes of Rothesay and Largs.

CLYDEPORT BUILDING, 16 Robertson St. 1886, *Sir J. J. Burnet* [**267**, *opp*]. The Clyde Navigation Trust was established by Act of Parliament in 1858 to promote and manage trade on the river Clyde. Burnet's imposing design (which he extended in 1905–8, incorporating the dome) is fitting for an organisation that rivalled the local council in power, wealth and influence.

[**268**] AMPHITRITE WITH A PAIR OF SEAHORSES, *Albert Hemstock Hodge*. The statuary and carvings on the Clydeport building are the most impressive in the city. Amphitrite was the wife of Poseidon – who was the brother of Zeus and Greek god of the sea – and the mother of Triton, the merman. [**269**] POSEIDON AND TRITON ABOVE ALLEGORICAL PEDIMENT, *John Mossman*. On the pediment Father Clyde is flanked by figures representing the eastern and western hemispheres.

Clydeport Building, 16 Robertson Street [see **267**]

[**270**] HENRY BELL AND APPRENTICES, *Albert Hemstock Hodge*. Bell took the maritime industry into a new age with his vessel, the *Comet*, launched in 1812, the first commercially viable steamship in Europe.

[**271**] THOMAS TELFORD, *Albert Hemstock Hodge*, APPRENTICES, *John Mossman*. Telford, born in Dumfries-shire in 1757, rose from humble beginnings to become one of the greatest architects and civil engineers in British history, building a plethora of roads, canals and bridges. His contribution to the development of the Clyde is recognised in this carving, in which he is holding technical plans under his left arm.

[**272**] DOCKERS. Highly appropriate for a building devoted to ships and the sea.

Clydeport Building, 16 Robertson Street

[273] ANTE-ROOM. In this plush apartment, with its walnut-covered walls, a portrait of Henry Bell, the father of steam navigation. Adjacent is the rectangular reception room (*not shown*), where there is a large meeting table, a wood carving with sailing ship and also carvings of Glasgow's coat of arms and the royal arms.

[274] SECOND TRUST HALL. Another elegant and sophisticated room, with maritime paintings,

walls panelled with French walnut and much stained glass. Windows afford excellent view of the Clyde. There is an old clock in this room known as the Regulator, which was connected to the other clocks in the building and controlled them. The white marble Ionic columns divide the room into eight bays.

[275] SHIPBUILDING. The three circular stained-glass windows represent shipbuilding, commerce and engineering.

[276] KINGSTON BRIDGE, 1970, *W. A. Fairhust & Partners.* One of the busiest road bridges in Europe, served by three miles of elevated approach roads and intersections. The main river span is huge, at 470 feet (143 metres). Gives motorists and their passengers spectacular views up and down the Clyde.

[277] CLYDE ARC, 2006. An unusual design in that it crosses the river in a skewed alignment, leading Glaswegians to nickname it the 'Squinty bridge'. Distinctive bow-string arch. The huge steel structure (*left*) is the Finnieston (or Stobcross) crane, 157-feet tall. Erected in 1931 it was used mainly to load heavy steam locomotives, a major industry at the time.

[278] BELL'S BRIDGE, 1988. Constructed to link the Scottish Exhibition and Conference Centre with the Glasgow Garden Festival and seen at the time as a temporary crossing for pedestrians and cyclists. Swings open to allow large vessels to pass.

[279] SCOTTISH TELEVISION STUDIOS, Pacific Quay, 2006. STV has been Scotland's leading commercial broadcaster since 1957, producing a range of programmes in areas such as local news, drama, documentaries and sport. Perhaps best known for its hit detective series, the long-running *Taggart*.

[280] BBC SCOTLAND STUDIOS, Pacific Quay, 2007, *David Chipperfield Architects/Keppie Architects*. Like its near neighbour STV, the BBC relocated here in search of spacious, modern facilities and its 8,500 square feet houses state-of-the-art broadcasting technology. Plain exterior but, inside, the huge central atrium is interestingly configured with terraces and platforms.

[281] SOUTH ROTUNDA, Mavisbank Quay, 1895. The Glasgow Harbour Tunnel Co. dug three parallel tunnels under the Clyde, two for vehicular traffic, north and south, and one for pedestrians. Two rotundas – on the north and south banks – provided access to the tunnels (north rotunda: **286**).

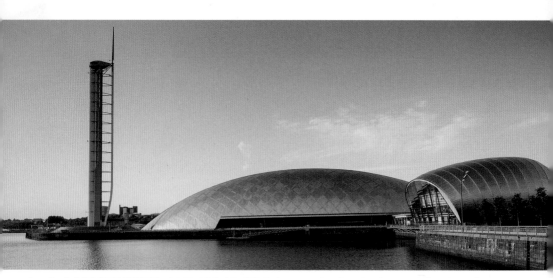

[282] GLASGOW TOWER, SCIENCE CENTRE AND IMAX CINEMA, 50 Pacific Quay. The 2001 Glasgow Tower (*left*) at 416 feet (127 metres) is the tallest free-standing building in Scotland and capable of revolving 360 degrees. Beset by technical problems but due to reopen in 2014. The titanium-clad IMAX cinema (*right*) has the biggest screen in Scotland at 62 x 82 feet and is part of Glasgow science centre (*centre*).

[283] GLASGOW SCIENCE CENTRE/WAVERLEY. Moored in front of the science centre is the *Waverley*, the last seagoing paddle steamer in the world. Named after Sir Walter Scott's first novel it was built on the Clyde in 1947 to replace the original steamer, which was sunk on active service during the Second World War.

[284] SCOTTISH EXHIBITION AND CONFERENCE CENTRE, Exhibition Way, 1985. The derelict Queen's dock was the site chosen for this purpose-built centre. Known to one and all as the Armadillo the design is much criticised but unmistakeable. A true Glasgow landmark.

[285] THE SSE HYDRO, Exhibition Way, 2013, *Foster & Partners*. With its 12,000 seats the Hydro – which cost £125 million to build – plays host to leading international rock and pop acts, as well as conferences and events. Based on Greek and Roman amphitheatres the use of translucent materials on the façade causes it to glow at night.

[286] NORTH ROTUNDA, 28 Tunnel St. 1895. One of the two historic rotundas on the banks of the Clyde serving the three tunnels under the river (south rotunda: 281). Access for carts was by hydraulic lifts; pedestrians used the stairs. But the tunnels were never a financial success although the pedestrian tunnel was still in use until 1980. Finnieston crane on the right.

[287] HYDRAULIC PUMPING STATION, Queen's dock, 1878, *John Carrick*. Formerly known as Stobcross dock, this was opened by Queen Victoria in 1877 and thrived until the 1950s when river traffic declined. Its hydraulic station powered a swing bridge over the entrance and also cranes. Simple box with pleasing Italianate tower; recently restored.

[288] HYDRAULIC PUMPING STATION, Prince's dock, 1894, *Burnet, Son & Campbell*. This dock would once have been busy with shipping but has since the 1980s been used for post-industrial purposes, such as the 1988 Garden Festival. The Romanesque power station survives and its octagonal chimney stump, which is now only one-third of the original height, has fascinating panels depicting the four winds.

[289] RIVERSIDE MUSEUM, 100 Pointhouse Pl. 2001, *Zaha Hadid*. The striking zigzag design of the roof, when viewed from above, is reminiscent of a wave and thus symbolises Glasgow's strong ties with the sea and ships. The 36-metre-high glazed frontage, shown here, provides abundant natural light for the three thousand exhibits.

[290] TALL SHIP. The ship in front of the Riverside is the *Glenlee*, a three-mast barque. Built in Port Glasgow, its maiden voyage was in 1896 and it went on to circumnavigate the globe four times.

Ships and the Clyde

It is a well-worn cliché that the Clyde made Glasgow and Glasgow made the Clyde. That does not make the old saw any less true. The river has served many masters and served them well: where would Glasgow have been without its swaggering merchants importing tobacco and sugar from far-flung lands, its legendary shipbuilders constructing more vessels than any other city on earth, its shipping lines transporting the fruits of its manufacturing industries around the globe? Even when Glaswegians were taking a hard-earned annual holiday it was to the Clyde they turned to go 'doon the watter'.

Strange then that the river was almost wholly unsuited to nearly every form of commerce: in its natural state it is shallow, in places less than two feet deep at low tide. It meant that until the early nineteenth century, many ocean-going ships had to unload their cargoes in Ayrshire, Port Glasgow or Greenock. Anxious to improve the Clyde's navigability, reports were called for, one written in 1805 by the great civil engineer, Thomas Telford, who advocated 'canalising' the river, a process that when completed allowed ships of up to 150 tons to dock in Glasgow harbour. This was followed by a number of measures that included dynamiting the river bed and continuous dredging. Eventually, by the second half of the nineteenth century, large ships could not only access the harbour but also be constructed and launched on the river.

The first great wave of economic activity on the Clyde was the importation of agricultural produce from the Americas, particularly tobacco and sugar. By 1771 Glasgow was importing 46 million tons of tobacco a year, and almost as much sugar. Many Glaswegians made considerable sums in the trade, others a good living. The more enterprising made huge fortunes, none more so than the four leading Tobacco Lords, as this breed of entrepreneur became known. Chief among them was Alexander Speirs (1714–82) who accumulated the largest business and was able to build a huge mansion in Virginia Street, invest heavily in land, at Elderslie, and to spend considerable sums on philanthropy. Another of the four was William Cunninghame, of Lainshaw, who built the most imposing mansion in the city, a mansion that would become the Royal Exchange.

If there is one trade that is synonymous with the Clyde it is shipbuilding. In its heyday, the sheer scale of the industry was staggering: by 1913 the Clyde – including Clydebank, Port Glasgow and Greenock – was producing 800,000 tons a year, a third of British shipbuilding output. Hugely profitable businesses were created and fortunes accrued to those entrepreneurs with vision and a propensity to take risks. Take Fairfields of Govan. It grew out of a yard

John Atkinson Grimshaw, *Glasgow Docks*

founded in 1858 by Charles Randolph and John Elder before assuming, in 1888, the name Fairfield Shipbuilding and Engineering Company. With the untimely death of Elder in 1869, William Pearce took the reins and the yard went from strength to strength. With four thousand employees it was for a time the largest private shipbuilding company in the world, its ships repeatedly winning the Blue Riband for fastest transatlantic crossing.

Their wealth accumulated, these titans of business did not neglect the communities in which they had prospered. Govan is testament to the extent of their largesse. There is the Pearce Institute, donated to the people by the widow of William Pearce, and Elder Park, which was given to Govan by John Elder's widow, Isabella, a noted philanthropist who did much to advance the position of women in Glasgow.

Many of the ships that were launched on the Clyde are now central to maritime history. In 1812, the *Comet*, the first passenger steamship in Europe, and based on plans by inventor Henry Bell, was launched at Port Glasgow by John Wood and Co. Then there is *Cutty Sark*, the legendary tea clipper, built for merchant John 'White Hat' Willis in 1869. The great liner *Lusitania* also emanated from the Clyde, in 1907, assembled by John Brown at Clydebank with interior design by Glasgow architect James Miller; at the time it was the largest ship afloat. On 7 May 1915, a day of infamy, the *Lusitania* was sunk by a German submarine, with the loss of 1,200 lives, almost all of them civilians. Brown's was also responsible for the two ships that set

Sir William Burrell

the standards for luxurious cruising in the interwar years, *Queen Mary* and *Queen Elizabeth*. Still in active service is *Waverley*, the world's last seagoing paddle-steamer, built in 1947 by A. and J. Inglis of Glasgow.

Glasgow was also a major hub for exports and imports. The city's manufactured goods went to every part of the globe, dropped into the holds of great ships by the huge cranes on the river bank, some of which, like the Finnieston crane, are still in situ today. The city's thriving economy around the turn of the twentieth century brought great opportunities for shipbuilders and shipowners. Men like William Burrell (1861–1958), *pictured above*, became fabulously wealthy, in his case because he revolutionised the so-called 'tramp-shipping' trade with his innovative business practices. Other companies moved not machines and raw materials, but human beings: Anchor Line, for example, prospered by transporting people to the Americas, Asia and Africa.

Not all the passengers leaving from the banks of the Clyde were going to such far-flung destinations. That great tradition of 'doon the watter' took hold in the late nineteenth century as Glaswegians headed for their annual holidays. Every Glasgow Fair the steamers leaving from the Broomielaw would be packed with holidaymakers eager to sample the delights of Dunoon and Rothesay. It is a tradition, of course, being kept alive today by the *Waverley*, which happily continues to ply its trade on the Clyde.

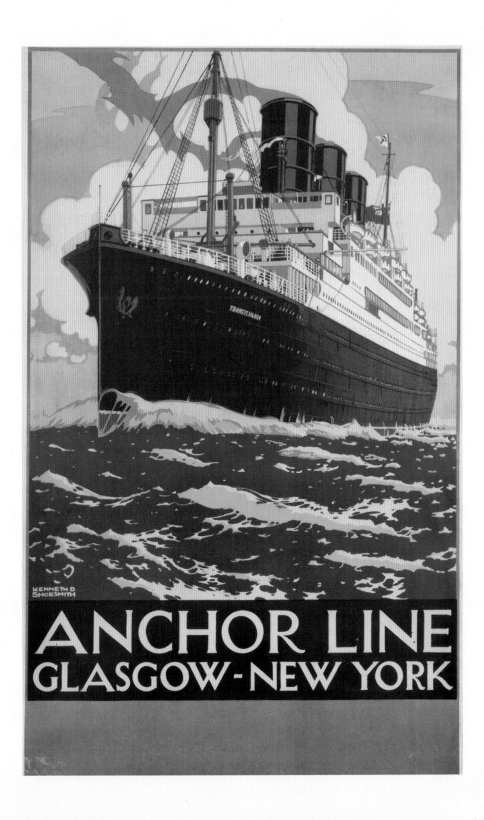

[291] ANDERSTON SAVINGS BANK, 752 Argyle St. 1900, *Salmon & Gillespie*. Glasgow-Style-cum-art-nouveau building now marooned from its contemporaries due to redevelopment. Wonderful panels, corner turret and mosaic doorway tympanum. Salmon was part of a three-generational dynasty of Glasgow architects; his best-known work is the Hatrack building [see **165–166**].

[292] CAMERON MEMORIAL FOUNTAIN, Sauchiehall St. west of Charing Cross, 1896, *Clarke & Bell*. Born in Dublin, Cameron (1841–1925) was medical student turned newspaper editor turned politician. He became a highly respected radical Liberal MP for various Glasgow constituencies and a leading light in the Temperance movement. Structure now sits at an angle.

[293] FITZROY PLACE, 1847, *John Burnet*. Site of Glasgow's first botanic gardens. Two storeys, end bays raised. An early work from Burnet (1814–1901), who was one of the city's leading architects, designing many outstanding buildings including Clydesdale Bank [**86**] and Stock Exchange [**92**].

MINERVA STREET AND ST VINCENT CRESCENT, 1849–58, *Alexander Kirkland*. Built as part of a proposed new suburb of Stobcross, with these two winding, Bath-influenced crescents. [**294**] The graceful curve of Minerva St. is particularly grand with a ground-floor arcade and Corinthian columns, giving the feel of a Roman temple. Sadly, the matching, southern section of the street has been demolished. [**295**] St Vincent Cr, with its distinct curve, is according to one historian, the 'most outstanding late classical terrace in Scotland'; a judgement that is hard to contradict.

[296]

[297]

[296] MITCHELL LIBRARY, North Street, 1911, *W. B. Whitie*. One of Europe's biggest public libraries with over one million items of stock, internet facilities, theatre, bistro and, as one might expect, extensive Glasgow holdings. Stephen Mitchell was a tobacco merchant who died in 1874 and left the bulk of his £70,000 estate to establish a large public library in the city. It eventually found its way to the present site.

[297–299] WEST FACADE, MITCHELL LIBRARY/ST ANDREW'S HALLS, Granville St. 1877, *James Sellars*. In 1962 St Andrew's halls, immediately adjacent to the library, burned down and the vacant site was used to extend the Mitchell, with Sellars's stunning façade retained. In his short life, Gorbals-born Sellars (1843–88) made a significant contribution to Scotland's built environment but his supremely confident St Andrew's Halls – heavily influenced by the work of Prussian architect Karl Schinkel – is his undoubted masterpiece. The huge sculpture groups are mainly the work of the ubiquitous *John Mossman* and include figurative programmes of **[298]** COMPOSERS, among them, Purcell and Bach, and **[299]** VISUAL ARTS AND SCIENCE, among their number, Raphael and Watt.

[300] ROYAL CRESCENT, 1849, *Alexander Taylor*. Handsome but uneven crescent on Sauchiehall St. by one of the city's less well-known 19th c. architects. Double Ionic porches worthy of note.

[301] FORMER FINNIESTON PARISH CHURCH, Derby St. 1880, *James Sellars*. This former Free Church place of worship is now in secular use but this is an impressive Greek Revival iteration by Sellars, who was responsible for St Andrew's halls, only half-a-mile away. Ionic portico gives it the feel of a Greek temple and the octagonal dome is a clever touch.

[302] ST GEORGE'S MANSIONS, St George's Rd/ Woodlands Rd. 1901, *Burnet & Boston*. Lacking the flair of Burnet's Charing Cross mansions, which are in the immediate vicinity [see **203**], these are nevertheless solid sandstone apartments built for the City Improvement Trust. The oriental-like turrets provide a talking point.

[303] ARLINGTON BATHS CLUB, 61 Arlington St. 1871, *John Burnet*. Britain's oldest private swimming club, run on a not-for-profit basis, with a wide range of facilities including a sky-lit, 21-metre swimming pool, gym, Turkish suite, sauna and steam room. Many of the original Victorian fittings extant. Burnet's original building single-storey but much extended.

[304] LOBEY DOSSER STATUE, Woodlands Rd. 1992, *Tony Morrow/Nick Gillon*. The eponymous Lobey was a legendary cartoon character created by Bud Neill, whose adventures, couched in Glaswegian dialect, appeared in the *Evening Times* from 1949–56. Lobey was the sheriff of mythical Calton Creek, on whose lawless streets he tamed outlaws like Rank Bajin.

[305] QUEEN'S CRESCENT, 1837, *John Bryce*. In this small area between Great Western Rd. and Woodlands Rd. there are several fine small-scale schemes, surely none more attractive than Bryce's classical Queen's Cr. with its handsome Doric porches. Awaits gentrification.

THE PARK AREA, 1850s–1860s. The layout here has been described as the finest example of Victorian town planning in Britain. The hilltop above Kelvingrove Park is dominated by *Charles Wilson*'s superb scheme, one terrace facing inwards (Park Circus) and the other facing outwards (Park Terrace). [306] VIEW OF SKYLINE. Park Terrace (*left*), Park church (*right*) and Trinity college (*far right*) combine to form a spectacular skyline. [307] PARK TERRACE, *Charles Wilson*. The first time that French Renaissance had been used on Glasgow houses.

[308] PARK CHURCH, Lynedoch Pl. 1858, *J. T. Rochead*. Sadly, after 1960s demolition only the tall tower remains of Rochead's church.

[309] PARK CIRCUS, *Charles Wilson*. The undoubted hub of the Park area; or Woodlands Hill as it is sometimes known. As Pevsner notes, its 'restrained and measured symmetry' demonstrates Wilson's 'subtlety and invention'. The house at no. 22 was built for Glasgow ironmaster Walter Macfarlane, owner of the Saracen foundry and later became a registrar's office; it is a particular delight and has stunning interiors by *James Boucher*.

[310] TRINITY COLLEGE, 31 Lynedoch St. 1857, *Charles Wilson*. Originally the Free Church college, and later part of Glasgow University, the three magnificent Lombardic towers make this one of the most recognisable sights on the skyline. Two floors with regular arched windows. Splendid central hall has been retained following conversion to residential apartments.

[311] WOODLANDS AND PARK AREA SKYLINE. Viewed from Arlington St. the three Trinity towers are split by the tall tower of St Jude's, Woodlands Road (*John Burnet*, 1875).

[312] CLAREMONT TERRACE, 1840s, *John Baird*. The centre property, no. 6 – now known as Beresford House – was originally a free-standing house in its own grounds before, seven years later, it was surrounded by curving terraces to either side. Imposing Ionic columns support the porches and the effect is greatly enhanced by fine cast-iron balconies.

[313] PARK STEPS, *Charles Wilson*. Many have argued that these steps, which lead from Kelvingrove Park to Wilson's fine residential enclave, should have been sited looking west. The great pedestals on either side of the steps have never supported the intended statuary, which would have undoubtedly enhanced their attractiveness.

[314] QUEEN'S ROOMS, La Belle Place, 1858, *Charles Wilson*. Designed as a concert hall with a number of smaller apartments. With the ambience of a classical temple, set off perfectly by the carved pediments and elaborate frieze, this must be one of the most aesthetically pleasing buildings in Glasgow. Non-contextual in relation to the adjoining houses, but this simply serves to accentuate the sheer ambition of Wilson's concept. Now a Hindu centre. **[315] FRIEZE**, *John Mossman*. Running round the east and north façades, Mossman's frieze not only shows the progress of civilisation from prehistoric man to the industrial age but also, in a fitting tribute, includes Charles Wilson to represent architecture.

[316] 4–5 LA BELLE PLACE, 1857, *Charles Wilson*. Short tenement cleverly designed by Wilson to emphasis the size and grandeur of the neighbouring Queen's rooms. Attractive carved ornaments above windows and doors.

[317] FIELD MARSHAL EARL ROBERTS MONUMENT, Kelvingrove Park, 1916, *Harry Bates*. Born to a military family in India in 1832, Frederick Roberts is one of the most honoured soldiers in British history. Awarded the Victoria Cross in 1858 for his heroism following the Indian Mutiny he rose to the rank of general and in 1901 was appointed commander-in-chief of the forces. This fine bronze statue shows him in pith helmet on his horse, Volonel.

[318] STEWART MEMORIAL FOUNTAIN, Kelvingrove Park, 1872, *James Sellars* architect, *John Mossman*, sculptor. Lord Provost Robert Stewart was a leading light in developing the city's water supply, much of which comes from Loch Katrine, where Scott's poem *Lady of the Lake* is set. So this exuberant monument – perhaps unsurpassed in Glasgow – has references to that work, notably Ellen Douglas, (Lady of the Lake) as well as a bronze of Stewart lower down.

Kelvingrove Park: Memorials and Statues

[319] HIGHLAND LIGHT INFANTRY, 1906, *William Birnie Rhind*. The HLI, or the City of Glasgow Regiment, can trace its glorious history back to 1787 and the 74th Highland Regiment of Foot or 'Campbell's Highlanders'. Since then the regiment has distinguished itself on many foreign fields, including at Waterloo and in the Crimea. This memorial, depicting a soldier in full battledress, faces the Prince of Wales bridge and commemorates men who fell in the Boer War.

[320] CAMERONIANS, 1924, *Philip Lindsey Clark*. The Cameronians derive their name from Richard Cameron, the 'Lion of the Covenant', and his regiment would become one of the most storied in the British Army. It is fitting that this wonderfully vivid war memorial was hewn by a man, Clark, who was himself a decorated hero.

[321] BENGAL TIGRESS, 1867, *Auguste-Nicolas Cain*. This was the first sculptural monument in the park. It shows the tigress carrying a peacock in her mouth, with which she is about to feed her two cubs. The statue was a gift to Glasgow from expatriate businessman John Stewart Kennedy.

Kelvingrove Park Statues

[322] LORD KELVIN, 1913, *Archibald Macfarlane Shannan*. William Thomson, Lord Kelvin (1824–1907) was for decades a professor of mathematics at Glasgow University (which he had entered as a student, aged just 11). One of our greatest scientists he is renowned for his work in thermodynamics and gave his name to the Kelvin scale of absolute temperature measurement.

[323] LORD LISTER, 1924, *George Henry Paulin*. English by birth, Joseph Lister (1827–1912) spent some of his professional life as a professor of surgery at Glasgow University, where he pioneered antiseptic techniques in surgery. Statue placed here despite originally being planned for the grounds of the Royal infirmary.

[324] THOMAS CARLYLE, 1916, *William Kellock Brown*. From humble beginnings in Dumfriesshire, Carlyle (1795–1881) rose to become one of the greatest literary figures of the Victorian age thanks to his essays, biographies, histories and masterful translations of German classics. Sometimes whimsically referred to as the 'Sage of Ecclefechan'.

[325] PORT SUNLIGHT COTTAGES, Kelvingrove Park, 1901, *James Miller*. This picturesque group of cottages is the last in-situ remnant of the Glasgow International Exhibition of 1901, which attracted more than eleven million visitors. It is a reproduction of a block of houses in Port Sunlight, a model township set up on Merseyside by industrialist William Lever.

[326] PHILOSOPHY AND INSPIRATION, Kelvin Way bridge, 1918, *Paul Raphael Montford*. The only major sculptures of this type in the city. There are four allegorical pairs on the bridge, one at each corner: *Peace* and *War*, *Philosophy* and *Inspiration; Navigation* and *Shipbuilding; Commerce* and *Industry*. Kelvingrove art gallery also in view.

[327] BANDSTAND AND AMPHITHEATRE, Kelvingrove Park, 1924, *possibly James Miller*. After seventy-five years of live performances the historic bandstand closed in 1999 and lay derelict until it was refurbished following a £1.8 million restoration programme led by Glasgow Buildings Preservation Trust (which does sterling work across the city). Reopened May 2014.

[328–330] KELVINGROVE ART GALLERY AND MUSEUM, Argyle St. 1901, *Sir J. W. Simpson & E. J. Milner Allen.* [328] Due to cramped conditions elsewhere Glasgow decided that a gallery worthy of a great city was required. Partly financed by the profits of the International Exhibition of 1888, with funding also coming from public subscription and the council, the end result was this exuberant, red sandstone, Spanish Baroque pile. Home-grown and perhaps more sophisticated designs were rejected – including a submission from a certain Charles Rennie Mackintosh – in favour of a plan by an English architect, which perhaps found favour due to its sheer bulk. One thing is certain: there is no other building in the city quite like it. [329] A side view of the art galleries with (*right*) Glasgow University, another prized architectural commission that went to an architect from south of the border. The bowling green was used for the 2014 Commonwealth Games.

[330] ST MUNGO AS THE PATRON OF ART AND MUSIC, 1900, *George Frampton.* St Mungo, who was born Kentigern in the 6th c, is the patron saint of Glasgow and the founder of an early Christian church on the banks of the Molendinar burn. Here on the north façade, above the central porch, he is depicted with a crozier in his left hand and with his right hand outstretched in benediction. Of the two female figures to either side of Mungo, one is reading a book (*left*) while the other (*right*) appears to be playing an organ.

[331] KELVIN HALL, 1445 Argyle St. 1927, *Thomas Somers*. Built to replace an earlier hall that burned down in 1925 the current Kelvin hall will probably be remembered by many Glaswegians as the venue for the council's Christmas circus and carnival. Now being transformed into a major new museum and research centre that will house more than 1.5 million treasures from city collections.

[332] ANDERSON COLLEGE, 56 Dumbarton Rd. 1889, *James Sellars*. The original Anderson's Institution, a medical college founded in 1800, was named after John 'Phosphorous Jack' Anderson, professor of natural philosophy at Glasgow Uni. from 1757–96, and, characteristic of a varied and colourful life, a soldier who fought in the Jacobite uprisings. Incorporated into the University in 1947.

[333] ENTRANCE: GLASGOW UNIVERSITY/WESTERN INFIRMARY, Dumbarton Rd. 1974, *Keppie, Henderson & Partners*. Behind the sandstone entrance looms the vast bulk of the Western's eleven-storey accident-and-emergency unit and main ward block. Concrete construction but mixed with white marble aggregate.

[334] FORMER QUEEN'S COLLEGE, 1 Park Dr. 1905, *Cowan & Watson*. Originally the Glasgow and West of Scotland College of Domestic Science, affectionately known to Glaswegians as the 'Dough School'. The college is now part of Glasgow Caledonian University while the imposing red sandstone building was taken over by the University of Glasgow and is now part of its faculty of education.

[335] FORMER WOODSIDE PUBLIC SCHOOL, 311 Woodlands Rd. 1882, *Robert Dalglish*. On a prominent corner site, designed in a Jacobean style. Adjoining, there is a large Italianate extension of 1896 built on an island between Woodlands Rd, Park Rd. and Eldon St. The earlier building is now a large pub/restaurant operated by a national chain.

[336] HILLHEAD PRIMARY SCHOOL, 110 Otago St. 2011, *jmarchitects*. The new school brought together four existing inner-city primaries on this site, which is within touching distance of both Kelvingrove Park and the river Kelvin. Radical, award-winning design with a distinct Scandinavian feel.

[337]

[338]

[337–340] MAIN BUILDINGS,
University of Glasgow, University
Avenue, 1866–86, *Sir George
Gilbert Scott*.

[337] Looking down from Gilmorehill over Kelvingrove Park, this 'Scottish Gothic' behemoth, the main building of the University, is for many people *the* symbol of Glasgow. The decision to appoint an English architect was much criticised at the time, as was Scott's subsequent design, not least by Alexander 'Greek' Thomson. Two quadrangles with dominant central tower and a spire added later by Scott's son, *John Oldrid Scott*. [338] The undercroft, or cloisters, below Randolph and Bute halls. Magnificent vaulting and columns, initial drawings by *G. G. Scott* but again finished by *J. O. Scott*.

[339] The main buildings from University Avenue. Founded by a papal bull in 1451, Glasgow is the fourth-oldest university in the English-speaking world. Located in High St. on the edge of the east end for more than four hundred years – in buildings that were Scotland's finest examples of vernacular architecture – a decision was made in the mid-nineteenth century to move from the Old College to the newly fashionable west of the city. [340] The baronial Pearce lodge, 1888, by *A. G. Thomson*, is a striking composition of fragments salvaged from the ruins of the Old College on High St, and paid for by shipbuilder Sir William Pearce.

[339]

[340]

[341] PROFESSORS' SQUARE, University Avenue, 1870, *Sir George Gilbert Scott*. Tall, rather plain, villas that were originally accommodation for dons but are now in departmental use. The great physicist Lord Kelvin [see 322] lived in no. 11 from 1870–99, as the plaque on the wall indicates.

[342] GLASGOW UNIVERSITY UNION, 32 University Ave. 1929, *John Arthur & Alan McNaughton*. Known to generations of students as the men's union, women were finally permitted to join in 1980. Renowned for the many debating prizes it has won, many top politicians cut their teeth in the debating chamber here, including John Smith, Sir Menzies Campbell, Charles Kennedy and Donald Dewar.

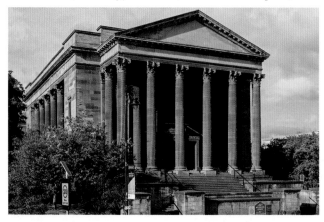

[343] WELLINGTON CHURCH, 77 Southpark Ave. 1884, *T. L. Watson*. Built for the United Presbyterians, the Greek-temple-like façade – with its raised plinth, exterior stairs and fine Corinthian columns to front and sides – is far from overwhelmed by the grandiosity of the Glasgow Uni. buildings that now surround it.

[344] HUNTERIAN MUSEUM AND ART GALLERY EXTENSION (1981, *William Whitfield*) AND MACKINTOSH HOUSE, University Ave. Founded in 1807, the Hunterian is Scotland's oldest public museum, with collections from the sciences and the arts, including the largest permanent display of the works of Whistler. The raised Mackintosh House (*left*) displays the interiors from his house at 78 Southpark Ave.

[345] WOLFSON MEDICAL SCHOOL, University Ave. 2002, *Reiach & Hall*. The imaginative use of this corner site, with its central atrium, won the architects prestigious awards. The University is renowned for its excellence in medicine, building on the work of pioneers like Hunter and Lister [see **323**].

[346] QUEEN MARGARET UNION, 22 University Gdns. 1968, *Walter Underwood & Partners*. One of two unions representing students here, QMU was formed in 1890 by women, for women, and until 1979 only women were accepted as members. The eccentric 1960s design, with projecting top storey, is perhaps not in keeping with the distinguished history of the institution.

[347] LILYBANK HOUSE, Lilybank Tce. c. 1850, *additions by Alexander Thomson*. Elegant mansion. The classical portico is an 1869 extension by 'Greek' Thomson for a later owner, publisher John Blackie. Another member of the Blackie dynasty, Walter, commissioned Charles Rennie Mackintosh to create the world-renowned Hill House in Helensburgh.

[348] 41–53 OAKFIELD AVENUE, 1865, *Alexander Thomson*. Attractive terrace that now requires attention. Recognisable Thomson flourishes in the twin temple-like pediments, square-column porches and mansards. There are some similarities to his Moray Pl. [see **575**], although on a larger scale here.

[349] GRANBY TERRACE, 2–28 Hillhead St. 1856, *William Clarke*. Mighty, forty-seven-bay spread with superb balustraded parapet. This is one of the earliest terraces in Hillhead, and one that architect Clarke chose for his own residence.

[350] WESTERN BATHS, Cranworth St. 1876, *Clarke & Bell*. Private baths with a distinguished list of former members, including businessmen like Blackie and Teacher. Symmetrical Italianate exterior with superb detailing inside.

[351] CURLER'S REST,
256 Byres Rd. 18th c. This two-storey cottage was built in the 1700s, although there has been an inn here for much longer. Such is its antiquity that there is a story, no doubt apocryphal, that King Charles II once visited and was so pleased with the service that he granted the publican a royal charter. The name derives from a curler's pond that was opposite.

[352] HILLHEAD SUBWAY STATION, 248 Byres Rd. The Glasgow underground, or the 'Clockwork Orange' in local parlance, was opened to the public in 1896 and now comprises fifteen stations on two lines, the inner circle and outer circle. Hillhead features an interesting mural by Glasgow novelist and artist, Alasdair Gray.

[353] BOTANIC GARDENS GARAGE, 24 Vinicombe St. 1912, *D. V. Wyllie*. One of the oldest surviving garages in Britain. Distinctive green-and-cream tiling is much admired. Recent successful residents' campaign to prevent demolition.

[354] SALON CINEMA,
17 Vinicombe St. 1913, *Brand & Lithgow*. Opened in 1913 as the Hillhead Picture Salon, with seating for more than seven hundred, a full orchestra and facilities to serve tea and biscuits to its patrons. Dome on west side and Glasgow-style features on the exterior.

[355] ASHTON LANE. With its clutch of trendy pubs and restaurants, and tucked in off cosmopolitan Byres Rd, this is one of the liveliest locations for nightlife in Glasgow. The Grosvenor cinema (*right*) dates from 1921 and has two screens, which, with their comfortable leather seats, have the ambience of private screening rooms.

[356] FORMER KELVINSIDE PARISH CHURCH, 731 Great Western Rd. 1862, *J. J. Stevenson*. Italian Gothic pile skilfully wedged into corner site, notable for tall bell tower with pyramid spire. The church's main sponsor was the leading Glasgow publisher John Blackie. The building is now an arts-and-entertainment centre, Oran Mor, which in Gaelic means 'great melody of life'.

[357] ST MARY'S EPISCOPAL CATHEDRAL, 300 Great Western Rd. 1884, *Sir George Gilbert Scott*. The first Episcopalian chapel was opened in Renfield St. in 1825 but the growth of the congregation meant that a bigger church was needed. So Scott, the best-known architect of the day, and the designer of Glasgow University [see **337**], was commissioned.

LANSDOWNE CHURCH, 416 Great Western Rd. 1863, *John Honeyman*. Converted to a theatre in 2014.

[358] Honeyman was an expert on medieval church architecture and this fine structure is clearly the work of a scholar. For Pevsner it is 'the most striking Gothic Revival church in Glasgow' and few could argue with that assessment. The astonishing spire is a conspicuous landmark on Great Western Rd: 218 feet tall, it is as elegant as it is slender and is greatly enhanced by *John Mossman*'s carvings. [359] The main entrance reveals superb attention to detail and pleasing symmetry. [360] In the apse, below the stained-glass windows, there is *Evelyn Beale*'s sculpted war memorial of 1923, in which Christ, with outstretched arms, is welcoming members of the armed forces.

[361] GREAT WESTERN BRIDGE, Great Western Rd. 1891, *Bell & Miller*. The best view of this superb late-Victorian bridge – the third crossing of the Kelvin here – is from the walkway underneath. Mainly granite, with steelwork by Sir William Arrol and decorative cast-iron with Glasgow's coat-of-arms by Walter Macfarlane. Lansdowne church is on the right [see **358**].

[362] CALEDONIAN MANSIONS, 445–459 Great Western Rd. 1895, *James Miller*. Like Kelvinbridge station, now demolished, this residential and commercial block was designed by Miller for the Caledonian Railway Co. Heavily influenced by the Arts and Crafts tradition, hence the extravagant domes, turrets and wide variety of window styles.

[363] COOPER'S BUILDING, 499 Great Western Rd. 1886, *Robert Duncan*. In its day Cooper's was one of Scotland's leading grocery chains. Its former west-end flagship, still a landmark here, is in the French Renaissance style with attractive cast-iron balcony, round-arched windows in different sizes and, best of all, the wonderful clock tower with observation platform.

[364] GLASGOW ACADEMY, Colebrooke St. 1878, *H. & D. Barclay*. Established by some of Glasgow's leading citizens in 1845 the Academy was originally located in Elmbank St. [see **194**]. It is still an independent school with a long list of distinguished alumni that includes Lord Reith, director general of the BBC, *Peter Pan* author J. M. Barrie and Scotland's first First Minister Donald Dewar.

[365] BELMONT CRESCENT, 1870, *John Honeyman*. A highly attractive semi-circular terrace with fine iron stairs. Glasgow-born Honeyman (1831–1914) is best known for raising the standard of church architecture in the city [see **8, 358** and **392**] but his work on other building forms was also impressive [see **140**]. He was also the first employer of one Charles Rennie Mackintosh.

[366] KELVIN STEVENSON MEMORIAL CHURCH, Belmont St. 1902, *J. J. Stevenson*. Looms large over the river Kelvin. Uses a variety of Gothic styles and is dominated by the huge north-west tower and crown steeple. London architect Stevenson designed a number of Gothic churches in Scotland [see, for example, **356**] but this is probably his finest. Excellent detail both inside and out.

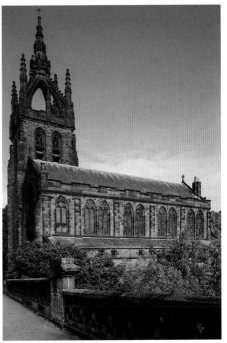

[367] RUSKIN TERRACE, Great Western Rd. 1858. Formerly St James Tce, this was built as two distinct halves with the east end more sophisticated and a storey higher than the west. Some ascribe the design to *J. T. Rochead* others to *Charles Wilson*.

[368] KELVINSIDE TERRACE STEPS, Kelvinside Tce. 1870s, *Alexander Thomson*. The 'sixty steps' were originally linked to the now-demolished Queen Margaret bridge. The retaining wall has a screen redolent of 'Greek' Thomson and a plaque explains his role.

FORMER BBC BROADCASTING HOUSE, 20 Queen Margaret Dr. The original part was **[369] NORTH PARK HOUSE**, 1869, *separately J. T. Rochead & John Honeyman*. Italian palazzo built as an art gallery for the Bell brothers, owners of a thriving Glasgow pottery, and later the BBC's Glasgow headquarters, while the addition is **[370] FORMER MEDICAL BUILDING, QUEEN MARGARET COLLEGE**, 1895, *John Keppie & Charles Rennie Mackintosh*. Part of the pioneering college established in 1883 to provide women with higher education and in 1895 incorporated into Glasgow University. The issue of Mackintosh's involvement in the design remains unresolved although the preliminary drawings for the project indicate that he was highly influential.

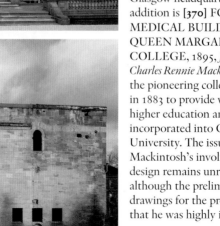

[371] KIRKLEE TERRACE, 1845, *Charles Wilson*. Originally known as Windsor Terrace, this is the first of Great Western Rd's many grand terraces and an early design by one of the city's greatest architects. Sitting high above the main road, it resembles a superb Italianate palazzo. Completed in 1864.

[372] KIRKLEE BRIDGE, 1901, *Charles Formans*. Linking Kirklee Rd. and Clouston St, this is for many people the finest bridge in Glasgow. Tall sandstone arches, pairs of Ionic granite columns and fine carvings, which include the city's coat of arms. Fine views from the botanic gardens.

[373] KELVINSIDE ACADEMY, Bellshaugh Rd. 1878, *James Sellars*. Although he never studied under 'Greek' Thomson, Sellars embraced many of his motifs in this design for the distinguished independent school. The temple-like front, the chimneys, the cast-iron lamp standards and the windows all bear the stamp of the master. There are elements too of *Thomas Hamilton*'s Royal High School, Edinburgh.

[374–379] BOTANIC GARDENS, 730 Great Western Rd. First located on Sauchiehall St, the botanic gardens moved here in 1842. The fifty-acre site is a delightful mixture of formal gardens, woodland and glasshouses full of exotic plants. [374] KIBBLE PALACE (*right*), c.1860, but re-erected here in 1873, after being donated by its owner John Kibble, on whose Coulport estate it originally stood. [375] PALM HOUSE. This is the tallest conservatory at 45 feet and it grows a wide range of tropical plants.

[376] KIBBLE PALACE INTERIOR (*top left*). Amid vegetation are found dazzlingly white Victorian statues, such as [377] KING ROBERT OF SICILY, 1927, *George Henry Paulin*. The subject matter is drawn from a poem by Longfellow and refers to an arrogant king who is deposed and has to take on the role of court jester, complete with monkey. [378] THE ELF, 1899, *Sir William Goscombe John*. This is a copy of a bronze original, which was shown at the Glasgow International Exhibition of 1901 and bought by the city council.

[379] HUMPBACK BRIDGE, 1908. Cast-iron bridge spanning the Kelvin, Glasgow's 'other' river.

[380] REDLANDS HOUSE, 11 Lancaster Cr. c.1871, *James Boucher*. A magnificent Italianate villa, said to be the largest ever constructed in Kelvinside. It was built for James Buchanan Mirrlees, a wealthy Glasgow manufacturer, on a site that once extended to twenty-four acres. For much of 20th c. it was a hospital for women.

[381] FORMER ST MUNGO'S ACADEMY CENTENARY CLUB, 998 Great Western Rd. 1877, *James Boucher*. A huge Italianate palazzo, originally called Carlston. It was built for another member of the Glasgow plutocracy, in this case James Marshall, joint owner of the Saracen iron foundry in Possil, which was also designed by Boucher.

[382] CLEVEDEN CRESCENT, 1876, *John Burnet*. One of the most elegant of the city's west-end terraces, in many ways it personifies *haute bourgeois* Kelvinside. Fourteen substantial two-storey houses linked into a terrace, with symmetry as the watchword. Double-house central pavilion; fine bay windows at ground-floor level.

[383] FORMER ASCOT CINEMA, 1544 Great Western Rd. 1939, *McNair & Elder*. Striking art deco suburban picture house that seated almost two thousand patrons. The semi-circular towers at the front enclosed stairwells. Became a Gaumont, then an Odeon, before transmogrifying into a bingo hall and has now been converted to housing.

[384] ANNIESLAND CROSS. Said to be the second-busiest (and perhaps the most complicated) traffic interchange in Europe, it links Great Western Rd, Crow Rd. Anniesland Rd. and a number of smaller thoroughfares. Typical red-sandstone tenement flats surround the Cross, including the highly regarded Anniesland mansions.

[385]

[385] ANNIESLAND COURT, 833 Crow Rd. 1966, *Jack Holmes & Partners*. At twenty-two storeys this narrow, rectangular tower block is a landmark building in these parts. It is the tallest listed building in Glasgow and the only tower block in the city to have been A-listed.

[386] GROSVENOR TERRACE, Great Western Rd. 1855, *J. T. Rochead*. Like Charles Wilson, Rochead was a draughtsman with 'father-of-Glasgow-architecture' David Hamilton. He found the inspiration for this wonderful terrace in Venice and it is all the more effective for its relentless repetition. After a fire at nos. 1–9 in 1978, skilful restoration work was carried out in steel and concrete.

[387] GREAT WESTERN TERRACE, Great Western Rd. 1869, *Alexander Thomson*. The most famous of Thomson's terraces and although it is monumental in scale it is in many ways the simplest and most restrained. Most of the houses are two storeys and basement, but with two-house-three-storey pavilions inserted one property from the ends. Magnificent Ionic columns and superb cast-iron work.

[388] GARTNAVEL ROYAL, 1055 Great Western Rd. 1843, *Charles Wilson*. Built as the city lunatic asylum this Tudor-palace design was competition-winner Wilson's first major commission. It replaced William Stark's radially planned asylum of 1809 in Parliamentary Road. Later became a leading private mental-health facility before being absorbed into the NHS.

[389] MAGGIE'S CENTRE, Gartnavel hospital, *Rem Koolhaas*. A support centre for cancer patients and their families based on the philosophy of the Scottish writer, gardener and designer, Margaret Keswick Jencks, who herself died from cancer in 1995. Striking single-storey building arranged around landscaped internal courtyard. Shortlisted for the 2012 RIBA Stirling Prize.

[390] KELVIN COURT, Great Western Rd. 1938, *James Fatkin*. Two H-plan blocks of luxury flats in an art deco style common in London's interwar suburbs but unusual for Glasgow, especially in the bold use of red brick.

[391] KENSINGTON GATE, 1903, *David Barclay*. Red sandstone, Glasgow Style houses in an elegant curving terrace. Superb bay windows on both main floors, complemented by fine stained glass, and baroque doorways. Viewed here from above the gardens in Victoria Circus.

[392] STRUTHERS MEMORIAL CHURCH, 52 Westbourne Gdns. 1881, *John Honeyman*. Formerly Free Presbyterian, another wonderful example of church-specialist Honeyman's Italian Renaissance style. The front pediment has four pairs of columns, Corinthian above, Ionic below, an undoubted *hommage* to Wren's St Paul's cathedral. Two bell towers with lead domes (only one visible here) and exquisite detailing both inside and out.

[393] CROWN CIRCUS, 1858, *James Thomson*. A remarkably confident debut by the 22-year-old Thomson following the death of his senior partner, John Baird. Sited at the top of a hill the effect of the convex shape is quite remarkable. It is an excellent example of his style before increasing Victorian affluence demanded large bay windows and more exterior detailing.

[394] TENEMENT, HYNDLAND ROAD. Built between 1890 and 1914 these substantial sandstone tenements with their prominent bay windows were built to accommodate the newly affluent middle classes. The stained-glass panels are probably by *Oscar Paterson Studios*.

[395] NOVAR DRIVE. Hyndland was one of the last parts of the traditional west end to be built, with most of it appearing in the late Victorian and Edwardian periods. Sometimes described as the 'tenement suburb', the vast sweep of Novar Dr. clearly shows the impact of this traditional form of Glasgow housing.

[395]

[396]

[398]

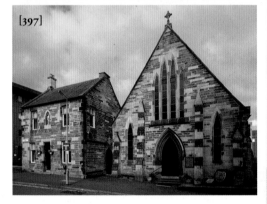

[397]

[396] RIVER KELVIN. The Kelvin has its source near Kilsyth, in the historic county of Stirlingshire and ends, twenty-one miles later, in the river Clyde at Yorkhill, after passing through much of north and west Glasgow. Here it is seen from Partick bridge. Its waters were used to drive Partick's many mills, most of them corn but also paper and iron.

[397] ST SIMON'S, 33 Partick Bridge St. 1858, *Charles O'Neill*. Originally an extension of St Peter's, Hyndland St. this simple Gothic church was used by Polish soldiers stationed at nearby Yorkhill barracks during the Second World War. Since then it has been heavily associated with that community, with mass still being said in Polish every Sunday.

[398] COTTIER THEATRE, 93 Hyndland St. 1866, *William Leiper*. Winning the competition for this, the former Dowanhill church, established Leiper's reputation. Standard Gothic design but the soaring tower, with pointed spire and open belfry, is one of the finest surviving in Glasgow. [399] Interior designs and stained glass by *Daniel Cottier*, after whom the theatre/bar/restaurant complex is named.

[400] WEST OF SCOTLAND CRICKET CLUB, Hamilton Cr. Founded in 1862 the club has hosted cricket matches between Scotland and top international sides and players of the calibre of Dr W. G. Grace and Sir Garfield Sobers. It was also the venue for the first football international: this took place in 1872, between Scotland and England, and resulted in a 0–0 draw.

[401] PARTICK BURGH HALLS, 3 Burgh Hall St. 1872, *William Leiper*. When the halls (which can also be seen in the centre of **400**) were built Partick was a proud independent burgh and would not be swallowed up by Glasgow until 1912. The bell-tower-and-cupola unit is noticeably off plumb.

[402] INVERCLYDE GARDENS, 137 Broomhill Dr. 1902, *W. M. Whyte*. Rare Scottish baronial tenement. White sandstone with much detail and the astonishing iron railings.

[403] SCOTSTOUN SPORTS CAMPUS, 72 Danes Dr. One of the best centres of its kind in Britain, catering to a wide range of sports, from football to rugby, badminton to athletics, and swimming to squash. Hosted the squash and table-tennis events at the 2014 Commonwealth Games.

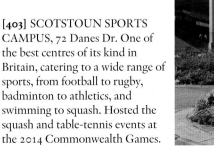

[404] VICTORIA PARK, Victoria Park Dr. North. At fifty acres certainly not one of Glasgow's largest parks, but considered by many to be the prettiest. The grounds encompass the fossil grove, more than three hundred million years old and surely the city's oldest attraction. The land for the park was given to Partick by Gordon Oswald in 1887 and later named in honour of Queen Victoria's golden jubilee, an event commemorated by the splendid **[405] JUBILEE GATES,** which were funded by the 'Ladies of Partick' and made at Macfarlane's Saracen foundry at a cost of £100.

[406] FORMER JORDANHILL COLLEGE OF EDUCATION, Southbrae Dr. 1913, *H. & D. Barclay.* The college, which operated here for close to a century until it closed in 2012, can trace its roots back to the Glasgow pedagogical institution established by David Stow in 1837, the first teacher-training college in Britain. Impressive red sandstone building, two large towers with copper spires.

[407] FIGURINES, 752 Argyle St. 1902, *Albert Hemstock Hodge*. *James Salmon*'s bank [see **291**] is one of the finest art nouveau structures in the city, greatly enhanced by the exterior decoration.

[408] MASONIC WALL PANELS, Two Fat Ladies at the Buttery, 652 Argyle St. 1869. This is an unprepossessing part of town to find one of Glasgow's oldest and most luxurious restaurants, all mahogany and stained glass on the inside.

[409] MYSTERIOUS CREATURE, St Jude's, 133 Woodlands Rd. 1875. The fine Gothic design is by John Burnet. The wild dog/cat carving is unusual in a church building [see **311**].

[410] GLASGOW COAT OF ARMS, Great Western bridge, 1891. One of several decorative cast-iron pieces on this bridge [see **361**].

[411] CHURCH ENTRANCE DOOR, 731 Great Western Rd. The Gothic influence is clear on what was Kelvinside parish church and is now Oran Mor [see **356**].

[412] GUARDIAN ANGEL, Kelvinside Hillhead parish church, Observatory Rd/Saltoun St. 1876. Delightful French Gothic church by *James Sellars*, beautifully decorated by carvings, especially its guardian angels.

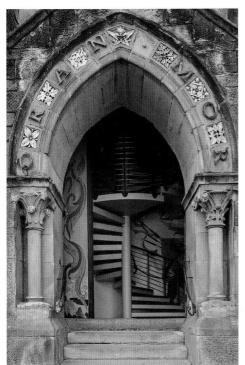

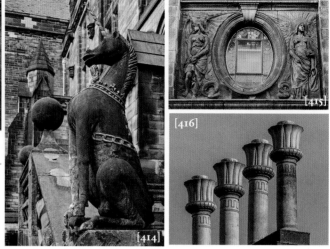

[413] OLD COLLEGE FRAGMENTS, Pearce lodge, University Ave. These fragments were salvaged from the University's Old College on High St. after it was demolished in the early 1870s and have been incorporated here [see **340**]. **[414]** LION AND UNICORN STAIR, west range, Uni. of Glasgow, c.1689. Another part of the Old College that was moved to Gilmorehill.

[415] WINGED FEMALE FIGURES, 56 Dumbarton Rd. 1889, *James Macgillivray*. Oval window flanked by mythical figures on the walls of Anderson college [see **332**].

[416] ROOF DETAILS, Lilybank House. A characteristic *Greek Thomson* detail on this extension [see **347**].

[417] KNOWLEDGE AND INSPIRATION, 16 University Gdns. 1960, *Walter Pritchard*. The old man, who presumably represents knowledge, is seated, while the androgynous youth is releasing a dove.

[418] PLINTH AND CROSS, Notre Dame high school, 160 Observatory Rd. completed 1953, *T. S. Cordiner*. This elaborate piece dominates the school's entrance tower.

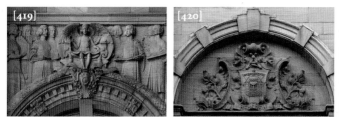

[419] [420]

[421]

KELVINGROVE ART GALLERY AND MUSEUM, Argyle St, 1901. The exotic baroque design of the art gallery [see **328**] is perfectly complemented by the rich carvings and detail on the exterior, in a programme supervised by sculptor *George Frampton*. [419] THE INDUSTRIES OF GLASGOW AT THE COURT OF MERCURY. The female figures are holding objects related to Glasgow's industries. [420] RENFREW, one of a series of thirty tympana with the coats-of-arms of Scottish counties. [421] RUBENS, one of several-dozen great artists immortalised in the spaces between windows.

[422] WHEATSHEAF, Bishop Mill building, 206 Old Dumbarton Rd. *unknown*. An appropriate symbol, reflecting Partick's connections to the milling trades.

[423] JUSTITIA, Partick burgh halls, 1872, *William Mossman*. One of three main roundels with mythical female figures, the other two being *Misericordia* and *Veritas*.

[424] RISE, Meadowside Sq. 2008, *Andy Scott*. Located next to the Clyde this six-metre-tall sculpture represents the spirit of the city and its people. It is made of galvanised steel plates, evoking memories of the great ships that were once launched from here.

[422]

[423]

[424]

[425] SMALL-ANIMAL HOSPITAL, 464 Bearsden Rd. 2009, *Archial Architects*. With a team of veterinary specialists, allied to state-of-the-art facilities, this is one of the leading establishments in its field. Located in the Garscube estate the striking and award-winning design ingeniously integrates the hospital buildings with their natural surroundings.

[426] KELVIN AQUEDUCT, 1790, *Robert Whitworth*. Completed in 1790 the Forth and Clyde canal's final stretch includes this spectacular aqueduct, which carries the waterway across the river Kelvin. When built it was the largest structure of its kind in Britain.

[427] MARYHILL BURGH HALLS, 10 Gairbraid Ave. 1878, *Duncan McNaughtan*. French-hotel-style building commissioned by the then proudly independent burgh of Maryhill. Used as a police station, court, jail and municipal offices. Comprehensively refurbished in 2011.

[428] QUEEN'S CROSS CHURCH, 866 Garscube Rd. 1899, *Charles Rennie Mackintosh*. A stunning combination of art nouveau and Gothic elements, this small church was commissioned by the Free Church in 1896. The eclecticism can be seen to best effect in the windows, which are Gothic but with a hint of modernism. It has the distinction of being the only church designed by Mackintosh and is now the headquarters of the Charles Rennie Mackintosh Society.

[429] RUCHILL CHURCH HALL, 17 Shakespeare St. 1899, *Charles Rennie Mackintosh*. A minor work, but, with its fine art nouveau detailing, one touched by genius and redolent of the Mackintosh style. Built as a mission hall for Westbourne Free Church.

[430] FIRHILL STADIUM, 80 Firhill Rd. Sharing a city with the Old Firm giants is no easy task but Partick Thistle FC has won two major trophies: in 1921 the 'Jags' beat Rangers to lift the Scottish Cup while Celtic were defeated in the 1971 League Cup final.

[431] RUCHILL HOSPITAL WATER TOWER, 520 Bilsland Dr. 1892, *A. B. McDonald*. This was Glasgow's second fever hospital, dealing with what today would be less common and more treatable ailments. Exuberant Flemish-style tower with turrets and domes.

[432] ST COLUMBA'S, 74 Hopehill Rd. 1941, *Gillespie, Kidd & Coia*. With its Italian Romanesque details this is an good example of the early work of church specialist Jack Coia. The only Glasgow church built during the Second World War.

[433] FORTH AND CLYDE CANAL WORKSHOPS, 1 Applecross St. c.1800. The oldest canal-related buildings in Scotland, providing a fascinating glimpse into Glasgow's industrial history.

[434] CITY OF GLASGOW GRAIN MILLS, 4 Speirs Wharf, 1851. The grain mills were built for John Currie and Co and had twenty pairs of stones and a condensing engine. The pleasing, two-storey Georgian house on the right served as the canal offices. Speirs Wharf is part of Port Dundas, which lies alongside the Forth and Clyde canal, and was effectively an early 19th c. industrial estate and Glasgow's most important port until the Clyde was deepened.

[435] PORT DUNDAS SUGAR REFINERY, 40 Speirs Wharf, 1866. The sheer size of these seven-storey premises emphasises the commercial importance of Port Dundas.

[436] ST GEORGE'S IN THE FIELDS, 485 St George's Rd. 1886, *H. & D. Barclay*. Replacing an older church on this site that was burned down, this beautifully proportioned structure was influenced by Alexander Thomson's classicism. The raised portico, with its six 28-foot Ionic columns, allows the superb façade to be fully appreciated. Superb sculpture, *Christ Feeding the Multitude*, by *William Birnie Rhind*.

[437] CLARENDON PLACE, 7 Maryhill Rd. 1841, *Alexander Taylor*. A great circus with two grand blocks facing St George's Cross was planned but only Clarendon Pl. was built.

[438] WOODSIDE LIBRARY, 343 St George's Rd. 1905, *J. R. Rhind*. Stylish, Renaissance-influenced design. In the pediment there are three naked female figures, surrounded by books. The group on the roof also features a female figure holding a book.

[439] TSB BUILDING, Shamrock St/New City Rd. 1906, *Neil Duff*. Outstanding use of the gushet between two streets. Fine baroque tower; rich detailing and carvings.

[440] FORMER DUNDAS VALE TEACHERS' CENTRE, 4 New City Rd. 1837, *David Hamilton*. This was Scotland's first teacher-training college, founded by educationalist David Stow, a man with surprisingly progressive views on how schools should be run.

[441] NATIONAL PIPING CENTRE, 30 McPhater St. 1873, *Campbell Douglas & Sellars*. Built as Cowcaddens parish church in a mixed Greek and Italian style. It is now a national and international centre of excellence for the Highland bagpipe and its music, with a school, rehearsal rooms, museum and library.

[442]

[443]

[444]

[445]

[442] ORIENT HOUSE, 16 McPhater St. 1895, *W. J. Anderson*. First use as a warehouse; later a model lodging house. Modern structure with steel beams and concrete floors but the facade has interesting Italian Renaissance detailing.

[443] ST ROLLOX WORKS, 130 Springburn Rd. 1887, *Robert Dundas*. Former offices of Caledonian Railway Co. Springburn was a major centre for the production of steam locomotives, with eight thousand people employed.

[444] SPRINGBURN PARK, Balgrayhill Rd. Park founded in 1892 on land donated by railway magnate, James Reid. Foreground: unicorn-topped column, formerly part of a Doulton fountain. Background: 1903 statue of Reid by *Sir William Goscombe John*.

[445] MARTYRS' MEMORIAL, Sighthill cemetery, 201 Springburn Rd. Commemorates John Baird and Andrew Hardie, weavers who were hanged following the Radical War of 1820. This was a turbulent period not only in Glasgow but also in other industrial cities, such as Manchester, where troops killed fifteen unarmed protestors in the Peterloo massacre of 1819.

[446] SIGHTHILL CEMETERY LODGE, 1839, *John Stephen*. Small, Greek-style building that resembles a temple.

[447] WALLACE MONUMENT, Robroyston Rd. 1900, *McGlashan sculptors*. The fine Celtic cross marks the spot where, in 1305, Sir William Wallace, Scotland's greatest hero, was betrayed and captured, before being taken in chains to London.

[448] STOBHILL HOSPITAL, 133 Balornock Rd. 1904, *Thomson & Sandilands*. A Poor Law hospital to which patients would only be admitted if they were classified as paupers, but later assimilated by the NHS. Prominent water tower with clock face.

[449] GARTLOCH HOSPITAL, Gartloch Rd. 1897, *Thomson & Sandilands*. Built as a 'luxury' asylum for fee-paying inmates, with separate blocks for the mentally ill poor. Huge, Scottish baronial cliff with two oversized water towers.

[450]

[451]

[452]

[453]

[450] FIREFIGHTER GATES, Maryhill burgh halls, 10 Gairbraid Ave. *Andy Scott*. The halls [see **427**] once included the burgh fire brigade.

[451] ST GEORGE AND THE DRAGON, St George's Rd/Maryhill Rd. 1897, *J. & G. Mossman*. Statue salvaged from the former Co-operative Wholesale Society building, which was nearby.

[452] PHOENIX FLOWERS, Cowcaddens underpass, 2010. The 'Metal Petals' are a colourful sight. Named for Phoenix Park.

[453] SPIRE VIEW STAR, Earlston Pl. 2012, *Rona McNicol*. The stainless-steel star's 'shadow' has drawings and statements by local residents.

MAIN ENTRANCE, FORMER NORTH BRITISH LOCOMOTIVE CO, 110 Flemington St. *Albert Hemstock Hodge*. The locomotive, [454], is an appropriate piece for this building, as is [455], *Science*.

[454]

[455]

ALEXANDRA PARK, Alexandra Parade. A popular east-end park dating from the 1860s. Much of interest including [456] MACFARLANE FOUNTAIN, a magnificent ornamental fountain with allegorical female figures that featured at Glasgow's 1901 International Exhibition. Designed by *David Stevenson* and constructed at Walter Macfarlane's Saracen foundry.

[457] ENTRANCE/ DRINKING FOUNTAIN WITH CHERUB, 1880. A typical example of a late Victorian fountain, located at park entrance.

[458] WD & HO WILLS TOBACCO FACTORY, 368 Alexandra Parade, 1953. Designed by company engineers this landmark building is now office units. Perhaps its main claim to fame is that much of the acclaimed film *Trainspotting* was shot here.

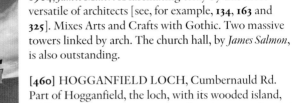

[459] ST ANDREW'S EAST, 681 Alexandra Parade, 1904, *James Miller*. A fascinating essay by this most versatile of architects [see, for example, **134**, **163** and **325**]. Mixes Arts and Crafts with Gothic. Two massive towers linked by arch. The church hall, by *James Salmon*, is also outstanding.

[460] HOGGANFIELD LOCH, Cumbernauld Rd. Part of Hogganfield, the loch, with its wooded island, is Glasgow's most important site for migrant and wintering water-birds.

[461] BLAIRTUMMOCK HOUSE, 20 Baldinnie Rd. 18th c. Plain mansion once owned by various members of the Monklands business elite and now surrounded by the large local-authority housing estates of Easterhouse. Bought by the council in 1954, it serves as a business centre with conference facilities and offices.

[462]

[463]

CRANHILL WATER TOWER, Stepps Rd. Built just after the First World War the landmark tower stored Loch Katrine water for the surrounding housing estates. [462] It is now even more of a talking point thanks to the ubiquitous *Andy Scott*'s sirens, which include (*left*) Poseidon, god of the sea, and a salmon (*centre*). [463] The tower was refurbished and floodlit in the late 1990s and apparently can be seen by planes en route to Glasgow airport.

[464]

[464] THE BRIDGE, 1000 Westerhouse Rd. 2005, *Gareth Hoskins*. Intriguing, award-winning building incorporating library, cafe, theatre, swimming pool and college.

[465] HEAVY HORSE, M8 motorway westbound, *Andy Scott*. Perhaps the best known work in Glasgow's new wave of public art and undoubtedly the most viewed thanks to its position next to Scotland's busiest road. Clydesdale horse made of galvanised steel bars, 4.5 metres tall at the head.

[466] PROVAN HALL, 15th c. Auchinlea Rd. The hall – one of the oldest and most historically significant houses in the city – was built in the Middle Ages for the prebend of Barlanark, a member of the chapter of Glasgow cathedral. Set within a park, Auchinlea, it consists of two linked buildings: the original medieval structure and an 18th c. addition. Now owned by the National Trust and run by the council.

[467] FORMER RAILWAY
WAREHOUSES, 105–169 Bell St.
1883. Massive, curving warehouse
facility constructed for the Glasgow
and South-Western Railway. In
common with many former
commercial buildings in this area
it has been converted to flats.

[468] LADYWELL SCHOOL,
94 Duke St. 1858, *John Burnet*.
Built as Alexander's school, for
James Alexander the owner of the
nearby mill [see **469**]. Italianate
design, asymmetrical tower, six
roundels with the heads of
prominent literati such as
Shakespeare and Milton.
Converted into offices.

[469] FORMER GREAT
EASTERN HOTEL, Duke St.
1849, *Charles Wilson*. Originally
James Alexander's thread mill but
perhaps best remembered as a
rather grim lodging house for
homeless men, which function it
performed from 1909 until the
1980s. Superb classical design by
Wilson, a great influence on
Glasgow architecture; the use of
iron and concrete apparently
making it fire-proof.

[470] KIRKHAVEN, 176 Duke St. 1857, *Peddie & Kinnear*. Built as Sydney Place United Presbyterian church in the Greek-temple style favoured by UP congregations of the time. Two superb Corinthian columns, fine carvings and surely one of the most impressive buildings in the east of the city. Now part of the same Wellpark/Kirkhaven enterprise centre as **471**.

[471] WELLPARK SCHOOL, 120 Sydney St. 1867, possibly *James Thomson*. Handsome Italianate building with a rather overbearing, and incongruous, tower. Now an enterprise centre.

[472] TENNENT'S MURAL, Wellpark brewery, 161 Duke St. Beer has been brewed on this site for centuries but the company's involvement started with brothers Robert and John Tennent who began brewing in this area in the 1770s, their premises becoming known as Wellpark. It now makes a variety of ales and ciders here, but is still best known for the flagship brand, Tennent's Lager.

[473] THE BARRAS, Gallowgate. Founded by Maggie McIver in the late 1920s this is the most famous flea market in Scotland and has become synonymous with Glasgow and Glaswegian culture. There was even a musical made about its history. Some say that the Barras name is a corruption of barrow, others that it derives from Burgh's Port, a gate in nearby Saltmarket.

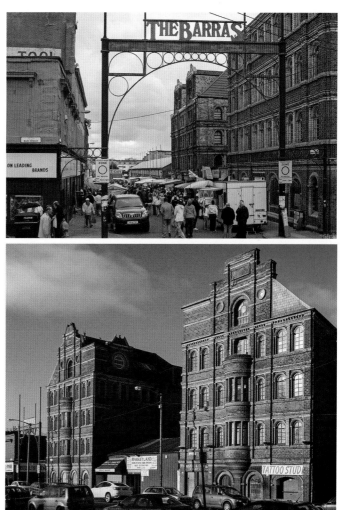

[474] CLAY-PIPE FACTORY, 10 Bain St. 1876, *Matthew Forsyth*. The manufacture of clay tobacco pipes was a major Glasgow industry in the 18th and 19th centuries, this facility being operated by William White & Co. Elaborate French Renaissance design in red and yellow brick, although, regrettably, the original centre block has been demolished.

[475] BARROWLAND BALLROOM, 244 Gallowgate. Above the units used for Barras market is found this atmospheric concert and dance hall, known for its excellent acoustics and distinctive neon sign. It attracted unwanted notoriety in the 1960s as the place where serial killer 'Bible John' picked up his three female victims.

[476] HIELAN JESSIE'S, 374 Gallowgate. This traditional Glasgow pub is on the ground floor of a tenement, built in the vernacular style, dating from the 1770s.

MEAT AND CATTLE MARKETS, Gallowgate. A major source of the city's meat supply in the 19th and 20th centuries. [477] MEAT MARKET ENTRANCE, Moore St. 1875, *John Carrick*. Imposing Roman Doric columns and pediment. [478–479] MEAT MARKET, Graham Sq. *John Carrick*. Two views of the former meat market, one showing how the façade has been retained. The arch to the right, with clock, is the entrance to the former cattle market. In **479**, the modern building on the right is the Matador flats (1995 *Page/Park*.)

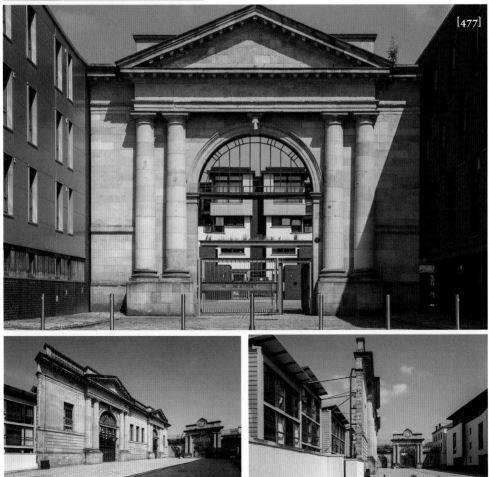

[480] PARKHEAD CROSS. Five streets converge on this busy junction, whose buildings are mainly from the Edwardian era. Parkhead was an old weaving village, which later became synonymous with two great institutions: Parkhead forge, a giant steelworks owned by William Beardmore, and Celtic Football Club, which has its stadium nearby.

[481] FORMER GLASGOW SAVINGS BANK, 1448 Gallowgate, 1908, *Honeyman, Keppie & Mackintosh*. Flamboyant, five-storey bank attributed to Keppie, combining Scottish Renaissance and baroque elements. Superb carvings by *A. Macfarlane Shannan*.

[482] ST PAUL THE APOSTLE, 1653 Shettleston Rd. 1959, *Gillespie, Kidd & Coia*. Fascinating, Corbusier-inspired composition by Roman Catholic-church specialist Jack Coia. Sculptor *Jack Mortimer* was responsible for the inspired artwork in the open tower, which is constructed in copper and depicts Christ's crucifixion.

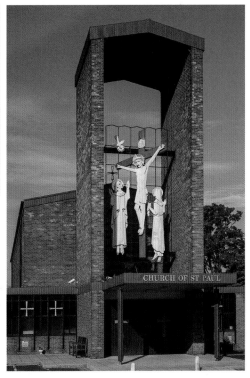

[483] SHETTLESTON HOUSING ASSOCIATION, 65 Pettigrew St. *Elder & Cannon*. This is a striking redevelopment of the Co-operative hall, an important community building in the Shettleston area dating from the early 20th c. The design won the prestigious Andrew Doolan Prize for Best Building in Scotland, 2010, awarded by the Royal Incorporation of Architects in Scotland. Although non-contextual the two buildings complement each other in a highly effective way.

[484] TENEMENTS, Tollcross Rd. The tenement – cheap and quick to build – is a housing form closely associated not only with Glasgow's built environment but also with the city's social history and culture. Most of those built in the 19th and 20th centuries have the same basic design: four storeys, a central close, common stairs.

TOLLCROSS HOUSE AND PARK, 591 Tollcross Rd. 1848, *David Bryce*. [485] Fascinating mansion house built for James Dunlop, a Tobacco Lord who later moved into coal and iron, acquired along with its estate by the council in 1897. Bryce – perhaps

Scotland's leading architect of the mid 19th c. – was a master of country-house design and helped to perfect the Scottish baronial style. Asymmetrical main block with low service wing. [486] The park is justifiably renowned for its rose garden and there are also winter gardens, nature walks and the Tollcross international swimming centre.

[487] DALDOWIE DOOCOT, Hamilton Rd. 1745. The doocot was part of the ancient lands of Daldowie, owned for centuries by the Stewarts of Minto. Distinctive curved roof; the interior had a unique ladder mechanism, allowing the pigeons to be collected for the master's table.

[488] BRIDGETON CROSS.
A major junction perhaps best known for its charming cast-iron shelter and clock, known locally as the Umbrella. The shelter dates from 1874 and was made by George Smith and Co. at its Sun foundry.

[489] FORMER OLYMPIA THEATRE OF VARIETIES, Orr St. 1911, *George Arthur & Son*. Billed as Glasgow's answer to the London Palladium the Olympia had seats for two thousand patrons. Later converted to a cinema and then a bingo hall it was extensively modernised and extended in 2011 and is now a library, offices and arts centre.

[490] CHURCH OF SACRED HEART, 52 Old Dalmarnock Rd. 1910, *C. J. Menart*. Interior reminiscent of Menart's St Aloysius [see **217–219**]. Extensive use of marble, for example in the fine Ionic columns. Ceiling, altar and stations-of-the-cross all worthy of note.

CELTIC PARK, Kerrydale St. Founded in 1888 Celtic Football Club, with its Irish Catholic heritage, is not only a leader in the field of sport but also one of the most important institutions in Scottish society. The Old Firm derby, contested with fierce Glasgow rivals Rangers, is considered the greatest club match on earth. [491] The stadium, much redeveloped over the years, now has a capacity of sixty thousand. [492] JOCK STEIN CBE STATUE, 2011, *John McKenna*. In 1967 Celtic, managed by Jock Stein, became the first British team to win the European Cup. The statue captures Stein with the trophy.

[493] EMIRATES ARENA, INCORPORATING SIR CHRIS HOY VELODROME, 1000 London Rd. At the 2014 Commonwealth Games, the state-of-the-art Emirates arena hosted the badminton events while the velodrome – named after Hoy, Britain's most successful Olympian, with no less than six gold medals – was the venue for the track-cycling programme.

[495]

PEOPLE'S PALACE AND DOULTON
FOUNTAIN, Glasgow Green, 1898, *A. B. McDonald*. [494] Aerial. [495] Ground-level.
By the 1860s it was recognised that the east end, at that time an overcrowded industrial area, needed a building to provide leisure facilities. The result was the aptly named People's Palace on historic Glasgow Green, with its museum, reading rooms, picture gallery and charming winter gardens. Its main function today is to tell the story of Glasgow's people. [496–498] DOULTON FOUNTAIN. Gifted to the city by Sir Henry Doulton it was first seen at the International Exhibition of 1888. It is the largest terracotta fountain in the world (46 feet tall and 70 feet wide) and one of the most remarkable products of the High Victorian era. The magnificent figures shown here (**497** *India* and **498** *Australia*) were inspired by the British Empire.

[495]

[496]

[497]

[498]

FORMER TEMPLETON'S CARPET FACTORY, Glasgow Green, 1892, *William Leiper*. [499] The vivid colours used in the brick, terracotta and sandstone façade reflected the carpets that were made inside and have made this one of the most recognisable and exotic buildings in Glasgow. Leiper was influenced by the medieval Palazzo Ducale in Venice, hence the factory's nickname of Doge's palace. [500] Fine details abound including the allegorical female figure that represents the textile industry.

[501] MCLENNAN ARCH AND SIR WILLIAM COLLINS MEMORIAL FOUNTAIN, Glasgow Green. The arch, dating from 1796, was the entrance to *James Adam*'s assembly rooms in Ingram St. but was moved after that magnificent building was demolished in 1893. *John Mossman*'s fountain of 1882 commemorates Collins (1817–95), scion of the Glasgow publishing dynasty.

[502] NELSON MONUMENT, Glasgow Green, 1806, *David Hamilton*. This 143-foot-tall obelisk is one of the few monuments specifically designed for Glasgow Green and was the first anywhere in Britain dedicated to Nelson's victories over the French, erected only a year after the Battle of Trafalgar.

[503] GREENHEAD HOUSE, 47 Greenhead St. 1846, *Charles Wilson*. Italianate palazzo built for cotton baron Dugald McPhail; later became the Buchanan Institute for destitute children and then a special-needs school. The 'studious boy' figure by *William Brodie* (*left*) was added in 1873.

[504] ST ANDREW'S BY THE GREEN, 33 Turnbull St. 1751, *William Paull & Andrew Hunter* (masons). One of the earliest Episcopalian churches built as such in the city and therefore anathema to the strict Presbyterian Glasgow of the time. It was often referred to as the English chapel (or the whistlin' kirk, thanks to its organ).

ST ANDREW'S, St Andrew's Sq. 1756, *Allan Dreghorn/Mungo Naismith*. **[505]** Said to be the most sophisticated church of its time in Scotland, it is still breathtaking today. Dreghorn was a wealthy businessman and enthusiastic amateur architect and he based his plans – which were executed by master mason Naismith – on *James Gibbs*'s St Martin-in-the-Fields, London. The magnificent portico is perhaps the finest in the city. **[506]** Grand interior with Corinthian columns and plasterwork in the rococo manner by *Thomas Clayton*.

[507]

[509]

[510]

[508]

[507] SEA MONSTERS AND SEA URCHINS,
Macfarlane fountain, Alexandra Park. An
example of the intricate decoration on this
fountain [see **456**].

[508] ALLEGORICAL FIGURES, St Andrew's
East, Alexandra Parade. Figures, art nouveau-style,
at the entrance to the church hall [see **459**].

[509] PHOENIX, Easterhouse Rd. 2000,
Andy Scott. Wire sculpture, symbolic of
Easterhouse's regeneration, just as the phoenix
rose from the ashes.

[510] BUFFALO BILL, Whitehill St. 2006.
The legendary Colonel William F. Cody, 'Buffalo
Bill', brought his wild-west show to Dennistoun
in 1891 as this statue vividly commemorates.

[511]

[511] THE COMMUNITY, Whitevale St. 1981, *Stan Bonnar*. Thought-provoking public art designed
by Bonnar with input from Dennistoun residents. Four naked figures: a girl, an old man and a middle-
aged couple.

[512] STEAM HAMMER, Westmuir St/Shettleston Rd. At one time William Beardmore's huge Parkhead forge employed twenty thousand men. This steam hammer, smaller than some used in the forge, is a one of just a few remnants from that mighty enterprise that can still be seen.

[513] TOWER, Bridgeton Cross shelter. Glasgow coat of arms and clock [see **488**].

[514] JAMES MARTIN MEMORIAL FOUNTAIN, Glasgow Green, 1894. Martin (1815–92) was a well-respected bailie and police judge. His monument was made at Walter Macfarlane's Saracen foundry in Glasgow.

[515] SPRINGTIME, Glasgow Green sculpture garden. First shown at Kelvingrove Park's *Sculpture in the Open Air* exhibition of 1949. Bronze Peter Pan-type figure, holding a pipe, with squirrel.

[516] CARVING, Hide, Wool and Tallow Market, 33 Greendyke St. This *John Keppie*-designed building dates from 1890 so the carving on the façade must have brought here from elsewhere.

[517] CALEDONIA ROAD CHURCH, 1857, *Alexander Thomson*. The first of Thomson's city churches, said to be his favourite, and indeed it was the place that he worshipped, as an elder, every Sunday. Realising the flat site would do little for the aesthetics he envisaged an impressive plinth, and put a 'temple', much resembling the Acropolis in Athens, on top. When the congregation asked for a steeple, he adapted an Italian campanile. The interior was equally impressive, but the building was reduced to a shell by a devastating fire in 1965. Despite many calls for complete restoration it is still derelict and, after much redevelopment in the area, very isolated. A masterpiece that must be restored.

[518] CITIZEN'S THEATRE, 119 Gorbals St. 1878, *Campbell Douglas*/1989 *Building Design Partnership*. Opened as Her Majesty's in 1878 but taken over by the Citizen's theatre in 1945, which had been founded by Scottish playwright James Bridie. Its mission today is to produce plays from the classic repertoire, along with new Scottish drama.

[519] GLASGOW SHERIFF COURT, 1 Carlton Pl, 1986, *Keppie, Henderson & Partners*. Huge, fortress-like edifice that does little to enhance its surroundings. It is Scotland's busiest court handling a wide range of civil and criminal matters.

[520] PARAGON, Old Rutherglen Rd. 2004, *Piers Gough*. Once a byword for inner-city deprivation the Gorbals has been transformed in recent years by new, and stylish, flats and houses. The Paragon, named after an old Gorbals cinema, is one of the developments that epitomises its rebirth.

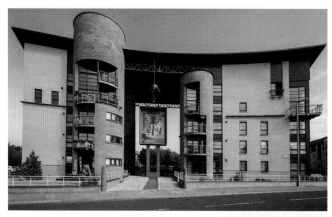

[521] KIDSTON TERRACE, 2001, *Hypostyle*. Another residential development that has made the Gorbals a sought-after place to live. The recent trend for sculpture and public art is also evident.

[522] HUTCHESONTOWN LIBRARY, McNeil St. 1906, *J. R. Rhind*. Refined, asymmetrical, French-style building with an impressive frieze – in which the carved figures include St Mungo – above the main entrance. Now in commercial use.

[523] FORMER ST FRANCIS FRIARY CHURCH, 405 Cumberland St. 1868, *Gilbert Blount/rebuilt Pugin & Pugin*. Tall Gothic church, typical of Pugin & Pugin, who also fashioned an opulent interior. Once home to the Franciscan order in Glasgow, it now operates as a community centre, while the building on the right has been converted into flats for the elderly.

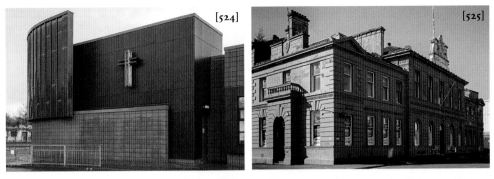

[524] GORBALS PARISH CHURCH, 1 Errol Gdns. 2011, *ADF Architects*. A dramatic, yet accessible, design for a building form that is becoming a rarity: a new, inner-city church. The original Gorbals parish church with its magnificent spire, by the great *David Hamilton*, was located in Carlton Place but demolished in 1973.

[525] POLICE TRAINING CENTRE, 71 Oxford St. 1892, *A. B. McDonald*. This was built as a police station, complete with court, cells and barracks. Palazzo style with interesting armorial on roof.

[526] SOUTHERN NECROPOLIS, 316 Caledonia Rd. 1848, *Charles Wilson*. Glasgow's southern 'city of the dead' contains the remains of around a quarter of a million people. The entrance arch is reminiscent of a Norman castle. Among the great and good buried here are Alexander 'Greek' Thomson, grocery magnate Sir Thomas Lipton and the architect responsible for the design, Charles Wilson.

[527] GLASGOW CENTRAL MOSQUE, 1 Mosque Ave. 1984. On the banks of the Clyde this is Glasgow's first purpose-built mosque and also the largest mosque in Scotland, with space for 2,500 people.

[528] CUMBRAE HOUSE, 5 Bridge St/Carlton Crt. 1937, *Launcelot Ross*. Large art deco commercial building, now offices, by an architect engaged to work on the Empire Exhibition of 1938.

[529] FORMER CALEDONIAN RAILWAY STATION, 36–54 Bridge St. 1890, *James Miller*. Before the development of Central station, Bridge St. was for decades the terminus for services from Ayrshire and Renfrewshire. The original, now-demolished station was a classical-style building of 1841 with a huge portico, while its successor was this fine, French-style structure.

[530] FORMER CHALMERS FREE CHURCH, 98 Pollokshaws Rd. 1898/ ABBOTSFORD PUBLIC SCHOOL, 129 Abbotsford Pl. 1879, both by *H. & D. Barclay*. The Italianate church has an unusual circular portico and fine stained glass; flanked by Roman-palazzo-style school.

[530]

[531] SCOTLAND STREET PUBLIC SCHOOL, 225 Scotland St. 1906, *Charles Rennie Mackintosh.* Overall plan fairly standard for board schools of the time but the Mackintosh treatment and details are characteristically original and innovative. The two Scottish baronial staircase towers, one each for the boys and girls, are a delight as is the infants' entrance. Now a museum of education.

[532] CO-OPERATIVE HOUSE, 95 Morrison St. 1895, *Bruce & Hay.* A massive French Renaissance warehouse deliberately conceived to be one of the most imposing buildings in the city, thus highlighting the growing importance of the Co-operative movement. It is said that the design was based on an unsuccessful competition entry for the city chambers in George Sq. but this was always denied by the architects.

[533] ANGEL BUILDING, 2 Paisley Rd. W. 1885, *Bruce & Hay*. Dutch Renaissance design, complex roof. Originally Ogg Brothers, a drapery warehouse, the building attracts attention because of the wonderful gilded angel on the roof, around which there has been much urban mythologising: the official title is *Commerce and Industry* and the sculptor was probably *James Alexander Ewing*.

[534] WALMER CRESCENT, 1862, *Alexander Thomson*. Deceptively simple terrace that repays careful study. Note the rectangular bay windows, the continuous colonnade on the top floor and the variations in the depth of the wall surface. One of Thomson's most impressive designs and similar in style to his Moray Pl. [see **575**]

[535] GOVAN TOWN HALL, 401 Govan Rd. 1897, *Thomson & Sandilands*. Govan, like Partick, was an independent burgh before being annexed by Glasgow in 1912. This huge, grandiloquent Beaux Arts composition speaks eloquently to Govan's civic pride and prosperity. It has recently been designated as Film City, a centre for Glasgow's film industry.

[542] LINTHOUSE MANSION, Elder Park, 1791, *Robert Adam*. This re-sited portico is the only remaining fragment of the Linthouse mansion, designed by Adam for James Spreull, a former city chamberlain.

[543] ELDER PARK LIBRARY, 228a Langlands Rd. 1903, *Sir J. J. Burnet*. Another building gifted to Govan by a wealthy shipbuilding family, in this case by Mrs Isabella Elder, wife of John Elder. Baroque details with some fascinating carvings [see **619**].

[544] ELDER COTTAGE HOSPITAL, 1a Drumoyne Dr. 1912, *Sir J. J. Burnet*. English Renaissance style. Intended as a maternity hospital hence the carving of a mother feeding a baby above the entrance.

[545] SOUTHERN GENERAL HOSPITAL, 1345 Govan Rd. 2014/15, *IBI Nightingale*. The original Southern General of 1872 (*clock tower in foreground*) was a poorhouse with the hospital wings added later. By contrast the new campus, due for completion in 2015, will have start-of-the-art facilities including thirty operating theatres, a fourteen-storey adult hospital with 1,109 beds and a children's hospital.

[546] CLYDE TUNNEL, *Sir Wm. Halcrow & Partners and others.* Two parallel tunnels, 2,500-feet long: one northbound to Whiteinch (opened July 1963); the other southbound to Govan (opened March 1964). They are now used by 65,000 vehicles a day and in addition there are separate tunnels for pedestrians and cyclists.

[547] LUMA TOWER, 510 Shieldhall Rd. 1938, *Cornelius Armour.* Former light-bulb factory with art deco motifs, built to coincide with the Empire Exhibition of 1938. The 84-foot glazed conning tower is a notable local landmark. Extensively renovated in the 1990s it now provides residential accommodation.

[548] CROOKSTON CASTLE, late 14th c, 170 Brockburn Rd. Set within 12th c. earthworks, this is the second oldest building in Glasgow after the medieval cathedral. When owned by the Darnley branch of the Stewart family it is said that Lord Darnley and Mary, Queen of Scots plighted their troth here. Later owners included the Maxwells of Pollok.

BELLAHOUSTON PARK is one of Glasgow's largest open spaces and has often been used for major events, such as the 1938 Empire Exhibition and visits by two popes.

[549] HOUSE FOR AN ART LOVER, 1901 *Charles Rennie Mackintosh/Andrew Macmillan*. In 1901 Mackintosh entered an architectural competition to fashion a modern house for a person of 'taste and culture'. The plans were not used in his lifetime but were later adapted by MacMillan, with building work completed in 1996. Wonderful interiors, with significant input from Margaret MacDonald, Mackintosh's wife.

[550] VICTORIAN WALLED GARDENS. The former kitchen garden for Ibroxhill House, which was demolished in 1914 with only the entrance portico still intact (next to House for an Art Lover). Wonderful blooms.

[551] PALACE OF ART, 1938, *Launcelot Ross*. This art deco block is the only building to have survived the Empire Exhibition. Mooted as a home for the council's art collection it is now a sports centre.

[552–556] POLLOK COUNTRY PARK with its extensive woodlands and gardens is not only a much-needed green lung but also a major cultural centre.

[552] POLLOK HOUSE, c. 1752, *possibly Allan Dreghorn or William Adam*. Large and impressive mansion-house built for the aristocratic Maxwell family, major landowners in this area. The main part (*seen here*), facing the White Cart Water, is rather austere but nevertheless well-proportioned and the later additions by *Rowand Anderson* from the 1890s also fit well. Superb interiors, enhanced by William Maxwell's unmatched collection of Spanish Old Master paintings by the likes of Goya and El Greco.

[553]

[553] PARTERRE GARDENS. The beautiful gardens are largely the creation of Sir John Stirling Maxwell, tenth baronet.

[554] BRIDGE ACROSS THE CART, 1758. Single-span arch with balustrade on parapet.

[555] WEIR AND MILL. 19th c. mill and power station, although the weir may be 18th c.

[556] BURRELL COLLECTION, 1983, *Barry Gasson Architects*. Shipping magnate Sir William Burrell (1861–1958) donated his magnificent art collection of more than eight thousand pieces to Glasgow Corporation in 1944. It took until the 1980s to build a permanent home, in this woodland setting in Pollok Park. As well as works by major artists like Rodin, Degas and Cezanne there are important artefacts from the ancient worlds of Greece, Rome and Egypt.

[557]

[558]

[559]

[557] POLLOKSHAWS BURGH HALL, 2025 Pollokshaws Rd. 1898, *Sir Robert Rowand Anderson*. Edinburgh architect Anderson was responsible for some fine Glasgow buildings, for example his station hotel, Grand Central [see **139**]. This magnificent example of his work – which is based on the Old College of Glasgow University in High St. – was paid for by the Maxwell family and gifted to the independent burgh of Pollokshaws.

[558] CLOCK TOWER, Pleasance St. 1803. This squat tower is all that remains of the former burgh buildings. Cairn (*foreground*) in memory of Pollokshaws-born John MacLean, socialist firebrand.

[559] ST MARY IMMACULATE, 150 Shawhill Rd. 1865, *William Nicholson*. Dignified Gothic RC church, later extended by *Pugin & Pugin*, with war memorial in foreground.

[560] POLLOKSHIELDS BURGH HALL, 70 Glencairn Dr. 1890, *H. E. Clifford*. Striking Scottish Renaissance edifice with dominant baronial tower. Scenically located within Maxwell Park; yet another gift from the Maxwell family to the people of Glasgow.

[561] MAXWELL PARK RAILWAY STATION, 1894, *Frank Colledge*. Attractive Victorian station in a shallow cutting originally owned by the Cathcart District Railway. Now a listed building.

[562] HAGGS CASTLE, 100 St Andrew's Dr. 1585. Former seat of the Maxwell family who moved here from nearby Laigh castle but moved on again when Pollok House was completed. Much restored and converted in the 1850s; ornate castellated style with intricate detail over the main entrance.

[563] BENEFFREY, 124 Springkell Ave. 1910, *William Hunter McNab*. Imposing Franco-Scottish design by the partner and successor of William Leiper, who was responsible for many fine villas in the west of Scotland. For many years it served as a hall of residence for the University of Strathclyde but has now been returned to residential use.

[562]

[563]

[564] CRAIGIE HALL, 6 Rowan Rd. 1872, *John Honeyman*. Plain yet refined mansion for Joseph MacLean, the son of William MacLean, owner of the Plantation estate. Interesting Italianate details and Ionic entry but distinguished by the outstanding interiors fashioned by *Charles Rennie Mackintosh* and *John Keppie* in the 1890s.

[565] SHERBROOKE CASTLE HOTEL, 11 Sherbrooke Ave. 1896, *Thomson & Sandilands*. Red sandstone, somewhat ostentatious, Scottish Baronial pile with tall tower that sits atop a hill. Grand central staircase.

[566] SHERBROOKE-ST GILBERT'S, 240 Nithsdale Rd. 1900, *W. F. McGibbon*. Built for the United Free Church, with the hall being completed six years before the church. French Gothic design, the statues at the entrance are of John Knox and Thomas Chalmers. Fine stained glass installed after a fire in 1994.

[567] THE KNOWE, 301 Albert Dr. 1853, *Alexander Thomson*. Earliest and least-known of Thomson's villas. More Romanesque than Greek with the round arches at the entrance perhaps influenced by his partner, *John Baird*. First iteration of the stylish chimneypots that would become such a feature of his *oeuvre*.

[568] KNOWE TERRACE, 553 Shields Rd. 1876. A long terrace, perhaps inspired by 'Greek' Thomson, whose Knowe villa is across the road [see **567**]. The graceful Gothic spire to the left belongs to *Robert Baldie*'s Pollokshields church of 1878 [see **569**].

[569] WAR MEMORIAL, Pollokshields church, 525 Shields Rd. 1921. Granite cross, 19-foot tall, honours the thirty-four men connected with this church who made the supreme sacrifice in the Great War.

[570] FORMER POLLOKSHIELDS WEST FREE CHURCH, 614 Shields Rd. 1879, *McKissack & Rowan*. Ionic-temple-style portico that owes a huge debt to 'Greek' Thomson. Corner tower reminiscent of *William Stark*'s city centre St George's Tron [see **91**].

[571] ST ALBERT THE GREAT,
153 Albert Dr. 1886, *J. B. Wilson*.
Originally the Stockwell Free Church it
became a Roman Catholic place of
worship in 1965. Italianate, very tall bell
tower; intriguing semi-octagonal
entrance vestibule.

[572] GLASGOW GURDWARA,
37 Albert Dr. 2013, *CRGP*. The first,
purpose-built, place of worship for Sikhs
in Scotland; able to accommodate
fifteen-hundred worshippers. *Gurdwara*
means 'gateway to the guru'.

[573] TRAMWAY THEATRE,
25 Albert Dr. 1894. *W. Clark*. Originally
Coplawhill tram works and depot and
indeed the first one thousand trams
for the city's system were built here.
Later became a transport museum and
in 1987 took on a third identity as a
theatre. The hidden garden to rear is
shown here.

[574] PRINT WORKS, 46 Darnley St.
1903, *D. B. Dobson*. Superb, Mackintosh-
inspired design for an art publisher;
firmly rooted in the Glasgow Style.
Prominent art nouveau features, for
example around the entrance doorway;
semi-naked female figure above first-
floor window [see **622**].

[572]

[573]

[575] MORAY PLACE, 1861, *Alexander Thomson*. One of Thomson's most stimulating designs, the standardisation of the architectural features – especially the colonnades on the upper floor – giving the terrace a strong sense of rhythm. The great man lived at no. 1, an end pavilion, with his wife, seven children, a nurse and a cook.

[576] SALISBURY QUADRANT, Nithsdale Dr. 1880. Late-Victorian, 'Greek' Thomson-influenced block but without the master's assurance, although the curved west front is noteworthy.

[577] LORNE TERRACE, 256 Darnley St/Nithsdale Rd. 1873, *Thomson & Turnbull*. Designed by Alexander 'Greek' Thomson's firm; building work completed in 1888, thirteen years after his death. Greek details on upper floors.

[578] ST ANDREW'S CROSS, Eglinton Toll. Where Pollokshaws Rd. meets Eglinton St. The large industrial structure to the right is the former St Andrew's electricity works, built for Glasgow Corporation in 1900, but now minus its two giant chimney stacks.

[579] GLASGOW SAMARITAN HOSPITAL FOR WOMEN, 69 Coplaw St. 1896, *MacWhannel & Rogerson*. Founded in 1886 in South Cumberland St. the hospital then moved to Tradeston before moving into this purpose-built facility. Mainly Arts and Craft design with art nouveau details.

[580] GOVANHILL PICTURE HOUSE, 47 Bankhall St. 1925, *Eric Sutherland*. With seating for 1,200 operated as a cinema until 1961, at which point it became a bingo hall and later a warehouse. Egyptian front with Hindu-style towers.

[581] GOVANHILL LIBRARY, 170 Langside Rd. 1906, *J. R. Rhind*. Single-storey, mainly baroque design, but with Ionic columns in the bays and main entrance. Wonderful statuary by *William Kellock Brown* [see **624**].

[582] SCOTTISH BALLET, 25 Albert Dr/ view from Pollokshaws Rd. 2009, *Malcolm Fraser Architects*. Studio, workshop, education and office spaces make up this fascinating modern building, which was purpose-built as a centre for professional ballet. Scottish Ballet, a multi-award-winning company, performs across Scotland and the UK and regularly tours abroad.

[583] FORMER HUTCHESONS' GIRLS GRAMMAR SCHOOL, 44 Kingarth St. 1912, *Thomson & Sandilands*. In 1639 Thomas and George Hutcheson, wealthy merchants, provided funds to establish a hospital [see **41**] and school. The school has been located in a number of buildings since then, including this girls-only establishment, which is now the primary department of Hutchesons'.

[584] DIXON HALLS, 656 Cathcart Rd. 1879, *Frank Stirrat*. Gifted to the burghs of Crosshill and Govanhill by ironmaster William Smith Dixon (1824–80), who took over the family firm of Govan ironworks in Hutchesontown after the death of his father in 1859. The works had five blast furnaces, which lit up the Glasgow skyline, leading locals to nickname it Dixon's Blazes. The halls are a frothy, yet charming, essay in Scottish baronial and still operate as a community centre.

[585] LANGSIDE PUBLIC HALL,
1 Langside Ave. 1847, *John Gibson*. This was
originally the National Bank of Scotland at
57 Queen St. but was re-erected here almost
stone-for-stone in 1901. Splendid Italian
Renaissance edifice by bank specialist
Gibson and made even more noteworthy by
the remarkable carvings. [586] COAT OF
ARMS AND DECORATIVE FIGURES,
1847, *John Thomas*. In the centre, royal coat
of arms flanked by a lion and unicorn and
on their outside female figures representing
Peace and *Plenty*. Note also bust of *Queen
Victoria* in the frieze below [see **626**].

[587] CAMPHILL GATE, 988 Pollokshaws Rd.
1906, *John Nisbet*. Interesting Glasgow Style five-
storey tenements with unusual flat roof, domes
and iron balustrades.

[588] QUEEN'S PARK, 520 Langside Rd. 1857.
Busy south-side park laid out by Sir Joseph Paxton.
Site of the 1568 Battle of Langside at which
Regent Moray defeated the army of his half-sister,
Mary, Queen of Scots, to whom the park is
dedicated [see **589–590**].

[589] FORMER LANGSIDE FREE CHURCH, 1896, AND BATTLEFIELD MONUMENT, 1887, Battle Pl. both by *Alexander Skirving*. Late 'Greek' Thomson-style church with impressive portico by his onetime chief draughtsman; now a bar/restaurant. Monument commemorating Battle of Langside [see **588**], topped by a lion with its foot on a cannonball. **[590]** BATTLEFIELD MONUMENT DETAILS. Intricate decoration: thistles, fleur-de-lis, swords and shields, and birds.

[591] GRANGE ROAD REST, 55 Battlefield Rd. 1915, *Burnet & Boston*. Charming Edwardian tram shelter and kiosk with green and cream tiles and domed clock-tower. Now a restaurant.

[592] GLASGOW CLYDE COLLEGE, 50 Prospecthill Rd/view Battlefield Rd. 2010, *Archial Architects*. The Langside campus of Glasgow Clyde, one of three in the city. Two very different buildings around a courtyard: on the left, five-storey main teaching block; on the right the futuristic drama-and-music building, which is clad in aluminium sheeting.

[593] VICTORIA INFIRMARY, 517 Langside Rd. 1882, *Campbell Douglas & Sellars*. The Victoria opened in 1890 and this was its administration block. Renaissance-influenced with flanking pavilions topped by cupolas. The coat of arms of Queen Victoria in centre and above them a puma [see **626**].

[594] NEW VICTORIA HOSPITAL, Grange Rd. *HLM Architects*. Purpose-built hospital that opened in 2009 and one of the best-equipped in the country. Based on the concept of a 'hospital-in-the-park' and designed to be light, airy and welcoming for the four hundred thousand patients who attend annually.

[595] FORMER CATHCART PARISH COUNCIL CHAMBERS, 183 Prospecthill Rd. 1907, *A. R. Crawford & Veitch*. Completed in 1907, five years before the ancient parish of Cathcart – named after the powerful Cathcart family – was absorbed into Glasgow. Symmetrical, single-storey, English baroque style with cupola. Now a health centre.

[596] DOUBLE VILLA, 25 and 25a Mansionhouse Rd. 1857, *Alexander Thomson*. Two villas with entrance porches on opposite sides, one facing east, the other west, a clever device that conveys the impression of a single house. Brilliant asymmetrical design with characteristic Greek and Egyptian details and the ground-floor bay windows may have been his first experiment in separating glazing from load-bearing structure.

[597] MILLBRAE CRESCENT, 1876, *Robert Turnbull*. Two-storey terrace often credited to Turnbull but may have been designed by his partner, Alexander Thomson, and built after his death. There are certainly Greek and Roman details and the cast-iron railings are another clue.

[598] RAWCLIFFE LODGE, 29 Mansionhouse Rd. 1861, *John Burnet*. Chateau-like mansion in the style of the Scottish Renaissance built for textile merchant and draper Alexander Stewart; said to have contained one of the largest picture galleries in Scotland. Became a Carmelite monastery in 1919, now residential.

[599] HAMPDEN PARK, Letherby Dr. On 17 April 1937 a crowd of 149,415 rolled up to Hampden to witness Scotland beat England 3–1. It remains the biggest crowd in the history of European football. The much redeveloped stadium (football specialist Archibald Leitch designed the original stands) can hold only 52,000 these days, but it is still the spiritual home of Scottish football.

[600] CATHKIN PARK, Myrtle Park. The original home of Queen's Park FC before its move to Hampden in 1903. The new occupants were Third Lanark, nickname the 'Hi-Hi', a proud club that won a league title and two Scottish Cups. Sadly, in 1967, it went out of existence and Cathkin is now a municipal park, with remnants of the original terracing.

[601] AIKENHEAD HOUSE, King's Park, 1806, *probably David Hamilton*. The first owner was tobacco merchant John Gordon and while it is only a probability that the original centre block was based on Hamilton's plans he was certainly responsible for the wings, which were added in 1826.

[602] CATHCART OLD PARISH CHURCH, 119 Carmunnock Rd. started 1914, completed 1929, *Clifford & Lunan/ Watson, Salmond & Gray*. Gothic with dominant square tower. Interior includes memorial chapel, some fine stained glass and art nouveau flourishes. Churchyard across the road has fragments of original church of 1831.

[603] CATHCART OLD BRIDGE, Snuffmill Rd. 18th c. The old snuff mill can be seen on the right but, despite its name, the manufacture of snuff was merely a sideline – paper making was in fact the principal activity of the Lindsay family, who owned the mill. Lindsay House is on the left.

[604] CASTLEMILK STABLES, 59 Machrie Rd. c. 1800. The stables serviced the mansion known as Castlemilk House, which was demolished in 1972.

[605] CARMUNNOCK VILLAGE. Carmunnock, which means 'the round hill of the monk', is the only village in Glasgow. Located between the city and East Kilbride it has a good deal of rural charm. Once owned by the Castlemilk estate and now a popular residential enclave.

[606–609] HOLMWOOD HOUSE, 61 Netherlee Rd. 1857, *Alexander Thomson*. Owner James Couper gave Thomson a free hand, a decision that reaped a spectacular dividend because this, in the eyes of many, is the finest house in Glasgow, the apotheosis of a great architect's philosophy.

[606] MAIN FAÇADE. The complex, Greek Revival exterior is brimming with original ideas: the almost circular bay windows, the magnificent cupola, the shallow roof pitches, the broad overhanging eaves, the complete asymmetry. The stunning interiors have been carefully restored and the building is now owned by the National Trust for Scotland.

[607] COACH HOUSE. Connected to main house by this wall, which helps to integrate the whole.

[608] CUPOLA AND CHIMNEY POTS. The ashlar cliff rises out of the hall to support the cupola, and is flanked by two of Thomson's characteristic chimney pots.
[609] FRIEZE. Impressive frieze and sculpted details.

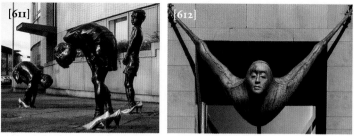

[610] DAVID, 517 Lawmoor St. Bronze copy of the famous *Michelangelo* statue.

[611] GORBALS BOYS, Cumberland St. 2008, *Liz Peden*. Public artwork based on a famous Gorbals photograph of three boys playing in their mothers' high heels by the legendary *Oscar Marzaroli*.

[612] THE ATTENDANT, Kidston Tce. One of a number of such figures here.

[613] BIRD SCULPTURE, Queen Elizabeth Gdns. Another thought-provoking piece of public art in the regenerated Gorbals.

[614] ALEXANDER THOMSON HEADSTONE, southern necropolis. 'Greek' Thomson (1817–1875) was one of Glasgow's greatest architects and a huge influence on his contemporaries.

[615] SIR THOMAS LIPTON HEADSTONE, southern necropolis. Ulster immigrant Lipton (1850–1931) opened his first grocery in Anderston at the age of 21 and through hard work and force of personality became the city's leading retailer.

[616] ALLEGORICAL FIGURES, Co-operative House, 95 Morrison St. 1897, *James Alexander Ewing*. Impressive group in the pediment including *Justice*, which is seated on a pedestal in the centre. The figure above the pediment is *Cybele*, mother of the gods.

[617] HOMAGE TO SHIPBUILDING, Bellahouston Park, 2005, *Jimmy Cosgrove*. Cast-iron-and-steel sculpture of shipyard worker.

[618] JOHN ELDER, Elder Park, 1888, *Sir Joseph Boehm*. Thanks partly to Elder (1824–69) Fairfield shipyard became the biggest such enterprise in the world [see **541**]. This fine bronze depicts him with his hand on a steam engine.

[619] GOVAN ARMS, Elder Park library, 228a Langlands Rd. 1903, *Holmes & Jackson*. Shield with carving of ship being built; flanked by carpenter and shipwright [see **543**].

[620] ZEPHYRS, Bank of Scotland, 816 Govan Rd. *Francis Derwent Wood*. Wonderfully imaginative sculpture of ship's prow with its sails being inflated by two zephyrs, which are blowing through conches. Note also the naked female figure at the front of the ship.

[621] HOGBACK STONES, Govan Old church, 866 Govan Rd. A unique collection of 9th to 11th c. artefacts, of which the most important are the five giant hogback stones, found only in areas of north Britain settled by the Vikings.

[622] MERMAID, print works, 46 Darnley St. *possibly William Shirreffs*. Part of the art nouveau detailing on this stylish building [see **574**].

[623] MASONIC SYMBOLS, Pollokshields burgh hall, 70 Glencairn Dr. The building [see **560**] included a room for the local Freemasons to meet in, hence the symbolism.

[624] PUTTI, Govanhill library, 170 Langside Rd. 1906, *William Kellock Brown*. The statuary on the face of this Rhind-designed building is particularly fine [see **581**].

[625] PUMA, Victoria infirmary, 517 Langside Rd. *James Mackinnon*. In urban myth the cat is said to be capable of healing other animals' wounds, just by licking them. The puma was adopted by the Victoria as a symbol of care. Royal coat-of-arms below [see **593**].

[626] KEYSTONE HEAD, Langside hall, 1 Langside Ave. *John Thomas*. One of a number of heads, representing rivers, on a building noted for its carvings [see **585**].

[627] SOUTHERN ARCH, Carmunnock Rd. 2000, *Rick Kirby*. Bronze statue of two female figures with hands joined together. Symbolises the regeneration of the Castlemilk estate and the importance of mutual support.

Index

GLASGOW FROM CATHKIN BRAES LOOKING TOWARDS BEN LOMOND

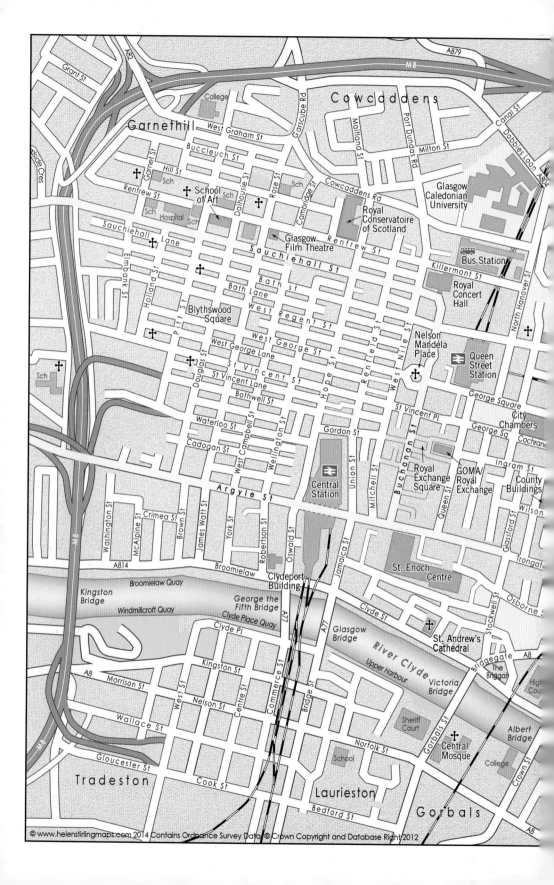

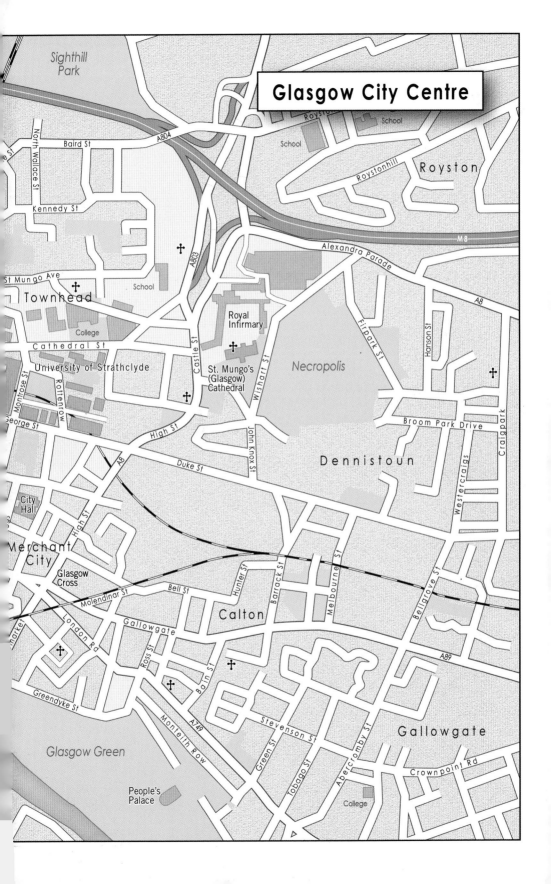

Picture credits: from the four essays entitled: Second City of Empire; Architectural Genius; Glasgow's Art; Ships and the Clyde. William Ireland, *Buchanan Street in 1910* (private collection). El Greco, *Lady in a Fur Wrap* (Stirling Maxwell Collection/©Culture and Sport, Glasgow, Museums). Margaret MacDonald, *The Heart of the Rose* (private collection). John Atkinson Grimshaw, *Glasgow Docks* (private collection). *View of the Library, designed by Charles Rennie Mackintosh* – main section, photo 208 (© Glasgow School of Art). Licensor for all five images: Bridgeman Images

Sir John Lavery, *State Visit of Her Majesty Queen Victoria to the Glasgow International Exhibition 1888*. Salvador Dali, *Christ of St John of the Cross* (both images © CSG CIC Glasgow Museums and Libraries Collections).

Park area aerial (© RCAHMS); Charles Rennie Mackintosh; Alexander 'Greek' Thomson (© Gavin Stamp). Licensor for all three images: www.scran.ac.uk

William Stirling Maxwell, Sir William Burrell, Anchor Line poster (courtesy University of Glasgow archive services, and, University Photographic Collection/Anchor Line Collection).

Books consulted: There are some excellent works on Glasgow's architecture, artists and history, including those by Charles McKean, David Walker and Frank Walker; Ray McKenzie; Sam Small; A. M. Doak and Andrew McLaren Young; Joe Fisher; Nick Haynes; C. A. Oakley; Irene Maver; Perilla Kinchin; Frank Wordsall; Peter Reed; Roger Billcliffe; and many others too numerous to list here. Special mention must be made of Pevsner's Glasgow edition, in the Buildings of Scotland series, by Elizabeth Williamson, Anne Riches and Malcolm Higgs.

Thanks to all those organisations that generously gave permission for the interiors of their buildings to be reproduced and to all those who provided advice and information.

Front cover, top row: SECC/SSE Hydro, Clyde view; second row: Glasgow cathedral, Templeton's carpet factory, Heavy Horse, Tolbooth steeple; third row: *Glenlee*, Glasgow University; fourth row clockwise from left: George Square, Hutchesons' Hall, Kelvingrove art gallery, Glasgow School of Art, Ca' D'Oro building; bottom row: botanic gardens, St Vincent Street church, Duke of Wellington statue, Mitchell library.

Back cover: top, Glasgow from Cathkin Braes looking west to Queen's Park, Govan, Erskine bridge and Kilpatrick hills; middle, Park Circus towers from Ruchill Park; bottom, Glasgow from Queen's Park to Glasgow University and the Campsie hills, with the Hydro and 'Squinty' bridge.

Front flap: Glasgow coat of arms, Royal Concert Hall; **Back flap:** lamp standard with Glasgow coat of arms, Cathedral Square.

First published in 2014 by Fort Publishing Ltd, Old Belmont House, 12 Robsland Avenue, Ayr, KA7 2RW. All rights reserved.

© James McCarroll and Duncan I. McEwan, 2014

All photographs on front and back covers and in main sections (numbered 1–627) by Duncan I. McEwan, except 208, *View of the Library*, Glasgow School of Art, details above.

Printed and bound in China by Imago.

Typeset by 3btype.com. Graphic design by Mark Blackadder. Glasgow city-centre map by Helen Stirling Maps.

ISBN: 978-1-905769-46-9